Erald Kaszlo

Philosophical adventures in Over 1001 reflexions

I0143072

SELF PUBLISHING
www.self-publishing.ro

Descrierea CIP a Bibliotecii Naţionale a României
KASZLO, ERALD
    Philosophical adventures in over 1121
reflexions / Erald Kaszlo; trad.: Briana Belciug –
Bucureşti: Self Publishing, 2014
    ISBN 978-606-8601-69-4

I. Belciug, Briana (trad.)

821.135.1-84=111

Tehnoredactor: Simona Bănică

ISBN: 978-606-8601-69-4

Bucureşti, 2014

Many things seem to be rubbish,
And that is because at that moment
We are preoccupied by other rubbish,
We are not yet convinced of.

The Blind Light within Ourselves

1. Happiness is a luxury that only those who do not want anything from life can afford.

❖

2. There are no atheist people; there are only people who have not yet found God.

❖

3. I have been gone round the world at lest fifty times on foot... in my city.

❖

4. There are moments in life when I would give everything I can for a moment of farewell.

❖

5. In old age, some people discover their inability and others their wisdom.

❖

6. If the woman gets bored, she will not stop until she will not bother us, too.

7. Only a dreamer has the opportunity to fulfill his dreams, the others live the dreams of other people.

❖

8. Freedom is infinite, that is why some people cannot perceive it differently than a way of discharge of their limited mind.

❖

9. To hide behind someone who is smaller than you, it means to stay on your knees.

❖

10. The relatively simple life is complicated every time, by some relatively square head.

❖

11. Every person (still) lives by the virtue of failed suicides.

❖

12. We think more than we can do, and we make mistakes more than we can believe.

❖

13. I have heard from an old man that health without money is pure illness.

❖

14. Since the castles have become some pitiable ruins, the invaders have become some joyful tourists.

❖

15. Life is not short, but memory is.

❖

16. To suffer, that is our mission. If we do not succeed, it will appear some kind person to help us.

17. Do not enjoy when you can pass through a wall... something is rotten: either you, or the wall.

❖

18. For the poor people the Bible is served as bread, and for the rich people, it is served as cake. The priests deal with it.

❖

19. The difference between an idea and wisdom is that, one can bring you some light for a moment, the other for all your life.

❖

20. Love is like a volcano; that is why you cannot oppose to it, nor postpone it.

❖

21. Some people become scarily sympathetic, revealing an exaggerated or inappropriate reason.

❖

22. To love, a smile is enough, to live together, it needs more smiles, more love.

❖

23. Everybody (is free) to think what he wants, but he should do the right thing.

❖

24. Good is an impression, and evil a statement, so it is better to stick only to the level of the impressions of things.

❖

25. Make of your job a small family; otherwise it will become a nightmare.

26. We are born from love and we die in its sin.

❖

27. Happiness is a reward for our good and praised deeds.

❖

28. The woman thinks she is so great, that sometimes she takes heels to believe it.

❖

29. It does not matter where you will end, in Heaven or in Hell, but it is important to get there with the head up.

❖

30. I think what other people have thought, as if I thought them, and I criticize what I have said, as if other people had said it. That is how smart I am sometimes.

❖

31. Who has patience and has nothing to do, he stays, and who has not patience search for other solutions in order not to stay.

❖

32. To love without limits, that is the true love... I mean to love all the women, never miss one.

❖

33. Life cannot be changed by any wisdom, but only by kindness.

❖

34. The past is a small compensation for the lost future.

❖

35. The intelligence of many women is hidden in the depth of different necklines.

36. Support your child in everything he wants to do; do not be malicious as all those in his age.

❖

37. Do not give the king the weapon, or the crown to the army.

❖

38. The ostrich does not shove its head in the sand out of fear, but in hope that in this way it can get away with it.

❖

39. Do not hold your hand too much; it may be cut.

❖

40. Dead people are not only in the cemeteries, but all around us on the streets.

❖

41. The original is unique, that is why it cannot be copied.

❖

42. Fear is human, but treason cannot be.

❖

43. I am flattered when it happens that somebody admires my woman... my trophy.

❖

44. How great the weather is today   perfect for a good sleep.

❖

45. It is better to give nothing to the stingy. No matter how much you give him, he will feel in prejudice.

46. Make the man be sorry for what he has done, not to get a rise out of him.

❖

47. Robbed by the humility to know that you exit and not to be able to do anything for it.

❖

48. I have not learned any vice that shortened my life, only my caducity.

❖

49. When you want to kill someone, it is better to start with yourself.

❖

50. The eyes do not see what the mind does not observe.

❖

51. Only after you pay, you have the right to repent.

❖

52. Fear is the damnation of the weak people.

❖

53. It seems I am not stupid all the time; sometimes I am a moron, too.

❖

54. Man is not alone on Earth, he is unique.

❖

55. Let`s not pretend easily from the others, from what it was difficult for us.

❖

56. By telling a single secret, one can lose its dignity.

57. Becoming an honest man, I remained alone.

❖

58. On the moment of our death we will take with us only what it belongs to us... behind us remaining only it unfairly belonged to us.

❖

59. We were born... even if we will die... because of our desire to live by any price.

❖

60. The people live along with the music they listen to. We live in times of musical slavery.

❖

61. Together with losing a friend, we also lose a part of our character, which he was keeping awake.

❖

62. For some people, the truth is an act of bravery, for other people, an act of brutality. It is rarely to see a truth born from an act of moral-honor.

❖

63. When you tell about a person what he has done, it is a discussion; when you start to assume, it is gossip.

❖

64. Oh... So cruel it is to taste from solitude next to your friends.

❖

65. You cannot lose what you did not... have. (Adam can say: "I have lost Eden". We cannot say it.)

❖

66. A man missing personality lacks courage.

67. Before surpassing the others, surpass you.

❖

68. We sometimes enter in a process of conscience from where we can hardly escape acceptable.

❖

69. Satan urges the people to sin not because he would not believe in God, but because he would be unhappy to remain alone in Hell.

❖

70. Among many other things, malice and goodness represent a real form of natural cosmetics. Just as malice succeeds in making us ugly, goodness embellishes us.

❖

71. The person, who is satisfied with anything, lacks two basic concepts: what is good and what is bad.

❖

72. Every bad day can be saved by a beautiful deed.

❖

73. J. RENARD says "if one had built the house of happiness, the biggest room would be the waiting room", but the longest line would be at the desk of complaints.

❖

74. It seems to me a real wonder to have so many force and vitality that to stay and do nothing, without going crazy.

❖

75. The value of life increases as soon as you start doing something.

76. Acting represents the art of not being a parrot, but a character.

❖

77. The war is not without scruples, but the treacherous men who support it are.

❖

78. The war is a dispute between two or more paranoid minds, which need to be taken and locked in a room, in order to approach themselves in tranquility. (quietly)

❖

79. If I had the opportunity to live again, I would refuse because I do not need to live again in order to realize that you cannot live without making mistakes. And if I had not made the same mistakes, I would certainly make others. I would not be incited by the idea of some new failures; there are too much those I already have.

❖

80. The smile is like a liquid crystal that shines in the darkness.

❖

81. I do not know what the importance of the Bible for some people is, but for me the most important is the human being.

❖

82. "Slave?! But who is not a slave?" "The person who is not feeling a slave." "Yes, but this does not mean that he is not."

❖

83. Every secret fractures the life in multiple parallel feelings.

84. How can you not have wishes, when you are permanently harassed by so many vital pains?! The pain represents the striker of the most impetuous wishes, to whom every human being gives up or dies.

❖

85. The love as a venom flows through the veins, not through the words.

❖

86. The lack of intelligence in a woman increases directional with the lack of indecency displayed.

❖

87. Love appears like fire... and when it disappears, behind it remains cinder and ashes.

❖

88. When escaping from the tutelage of the ideas, you start to discover among many other things an extremely important thing: the false headaches.

❖

89. Hell cannot be bad for anybody, but only right... without roundabout ways.

❖

90. We will all reach to heaven, but in the opposite way to that lived on earth. Heaven and Hell proving to be too little for the variable range of possibilities that would have been after death. Heaven or Hell being either too much or too little for each of us.

❖

91. Reconciling with a wretch, he will wreck you again.

92. Reconciling with yourself – it is a first step to a mental trick that we should prove in order to live. Then, one by one follows.

❖

93. Man does not live thanks to a virtue, but only to a unique wonder – the birth.

❖

94. In the cemeteries there are not dead people, but only bones and crosses... the dead people have rotten a long time ago.

❖

95. I sympathize very well with everybody, until I argue with them.

❖

96. It is much easier to deny something abusive than to examine it successively.

❖

97. I wonder who would have more need of forgiveness: Me (the all-unknowing) or God (the All-knowing)?!

❖

98. Everything a man does have as a decisive factor the will, including the laziness.

❖

99. There are old people who give as pretext the white hair instead of the mind inside the head.

❖

100. Any idea searches its relief under a warm sunray of a clean conscience.

101. An old man once told me that, when your soul hurts, it means it is curing, it means you still have it.

❖

102. Through the veil of memories, I watch the dawn empty of any chance, I am sequestered... by a damn hope. My heart rises on the sky and the sun in my chest, I cannot see any escape but in my soul. If there were some time now and now never, the wildness would stay as truth... and reward.

A small stop of a lifetime

II

103. When God will watch the people and He will start having headaches, He will already realize that actually He is watching in the mirror.

❖

104. The appearances are those that succeed in making us human. (in maintaining us)

❖

105. The law is good until you break it.

❖

106. The most appropriate revenge is the success.

❖

107. I support to you my opinion, too.

❖

108. I do not like... inedible flowers. It seems silly to me to break some flowers, and let them dry in a vase.

❖

109. The human being does not fear the loneliness, but the freedom this loneliness gives him... unknowing what to do with it, he is bored to death.

110. When our greatest dreams will resume at a simple sunrise, we can quietly light our own candle.

❖

111. The meaning of life is not in a certain thing that we do, but in everything that we do, and it keeps us alive.

❖

112. On the top usually arrive the gaudy things, because the stupid people represent the majority. That is why it is better to use a competent jury that the public opinion.

❖

113. The person who hangs himself executes a simple formality, since he is already dead at least five minutes before.

❖

114. There is no reason to do a bad thing, only for the villains.

❖

115. The praises and the offerings flatter a wicked soul, which is why the Devil always motivates its deeds; probably somebody will ever confuse it with a good god.

❖

116. Fewer explanations, even fewer complications.

❖

117. We thing freely, or at least this is what we believe.

❖

118. A smart person is the person who has never given you the occasion to know him. (judge)

119. When you are up you see many things – but poorly, and when you are down you see very well – but fewer thing.

❖

120. A friend is the person who protects you from stupid things, not that person who leads you to them.

❖

121. You cannot start anything that is not to the detriment of another thing. Therefore, when we do nothing, it cannot be but to the detriment of every things.

❖

122. Life will always have a meaning, even if it is just to live.

❖

123. The person, who does not know his diseases, has great chances to die a healthy person.

❖

124. Not every thought is an idea, and not everything that is original is also valuable.

❖

125. When the reason for which you stay with the person next you is discerned, you will be terrified. Not because of that reason, but because of all the other reasons that are missing.

❖

126. It is no wonder that we do not understand. We live in the same time, but in different ages.

❖

127. If you get married, you lose the trust of a woman, but you earn the other women`s trust.

128. His soul is so dirty that it dirties his clothes, and his hands as well.

❖

129. Happiness indicates us a more graceful way in which we can suffer. I do not see why we would ignore this aspect.

❖

130. Who cannot wish for at least one thing, will not be satisfied by any.

❖

131. If I had known I will become a billionaire, I would have worked for no hour, I would have suffered for no minute, I would have skipped and I would have starved happily ... all my life. If I had known... I would have been happy.

❖

132. The best friends cannot be but "one"... and this one it would be sometimes to be "too many".

❖

133. When somebody wants to seem original, he will come up with another stupid idea.

❖

134. The loneliness is not that terrible, but on the moment when you notice, before going to sleep, how empty the bed can be.

❖

135. The original exists only in the nature; the rest is nothing else but some subtle reformulations, rehabilitations, adaptations.

136. Do not condemn the atheist in the place of the sinner!

❖

137. The good man is good because he cannot be otherwise, not necessarily because he would not want to be evil.

❖

138. There are not the people who turn the back on church; it is the church that does not know anymore to make itself loved.

❖

139. It seems that the majority is looking for an ideal friend, whom it can fool and gossip as it wants, without offense... a silly dog.

❖

140. A person is so sensitive that it is impossible to bother him with something... especially when you succeed in existing.

❖

141. The greatest good is that good that you do not feel.

❖

142. The honest hearts beat in the same rhythm... wherever they are.

❖

143. It seems that the countrymen do not live only in the countryside.

❖

144. Do not give up before you try.

❖

145. The word gives us the science of everything.

146. We like life so much that we will grow old happily for it.

❖

147. The genius is unique. Stupidity and intelligence are common.

❖

148. How shameful it could be for somebody to "kiss your ass" in front of other people.

❖

149. The old age helps us not to die so alive.

❖

150. It seems that not all the angels have big wings, and not all the donkeys have big ears.

❖

151. Even if I fought with nobody, I do not speak with many people.

❖

152. Without nobility, love is filthy.

❖

153. The lack of positive energy of thoughts threatens our spiritual welfare.

❖

154. What is not under the sign of doubt lies below the indolence.

❖

155. I lost the battle with her from the first moment we saw each other: she shot me dead in the heart with an irrevocably smile.

156. In my way, I prove myself perfect... simply perfect.

❖

157. By using sad thoughts you cannot face life successfully.

❖

158. How large the field is, the eyes fly in color here and there with a willowy memory that rascally awakens to me a fresh youth.

❖

159. How great it is to have friends with which you have fun... and just fun.

❖

160. When we have had enough sex, we pass to more serious things, too.

❖

161. There is no greater lie, than this life.

❖

162. People are so mean that they can seldom surpass me.

❖

163. Your friend has a friend, which friend has another friend, and that is how the words fly. What do you think?!

❖

164. When we want to repeat a story, we are like a dog that is turning over its own tail.

❖

165. A room where it is only a bed along the walls. What greater love could you give to a woman?

166. Enjoy the little things! Being free, nobody fights for them. Being many, one can find them at every step.

❖

167. Rare pleasure maintains life bitter.

❖

168. We are the compass that draws the circle around our life.

❖

169. Not falling in sin or entering the water without getting wet.

❖

170. And this is how, a man stumbling into trouble, could die happy.

❖

171. If he had not have lived, while I was living, I would have been convinced that he reincarnated in me; now I have just doubts.

❖

172. Only when we love, we realize that we do not own anything, which is why it happens to offer everything.

❖

173. I cannot think something, without getting older with another forty years. I cannot think more... .this thing would kill me.

❖

174. Smaller is one thing, be happy, greater is one thing, do not regret, for being happy.

175. I am disappointed in consequence... aimlessly and maybe in this way I will succeed in discovering what the pain keeps hiding from me.

❖

176. If nothing it is and we still will not know.

❖

177. Developing that elegant position, where you accept all the bagatelles in life... pretending you also love them

❖

178. Giving everything, even if for a good moment of secondary importance.

❖

179. God has the opportunity to show Himself, and we have the opportunity to see us.

❖

180. Through a continuous care, life can become fair through kindness.

❖

181. Sometimes it happens that I study thoroughly... the inborn intelligence of some feminine feet.

❖

182. The greedy shakes the entire tree, just to eat one apple.

❖

183. Covered by the cloak of humility, I contemplate the success of nothingness.

❖

184. Now that you have promised, give him... Some other time, remember not to promise foolishly.

185. "I cannot come out, I have to work."/ "What do you work?"/"I stay."

❖

186. A dollar means nothing, but if you do not have it, it means a lot.

❖

187. The words begin to seem to me a poor expression of our failed actions.

❖

188. To a summer sufferance it fits a seaside love.

❖

189. There is no love without sighs.

❖

190. We hang down below an abyss, to which we will not find the end but in our soul. It keeps coming here, like elsewhere, all the things that separate us from our unique justice. The flowers shine at dawn, even if you died, against you and everybody else, the life will reborn again, thrill after thrill.

Prisoner inside the words

III

191. Intelligence is free from nature; do not protect yourself from thinking.

❖

192. The creation is stabilized according to the spiritual freedom of everybody and his visionary capacity.

❖

193. To be able to be appreciated as much as they want your best.

❖

194. The greatest good of a person is to be able to feel good... not only with him.

❖

195. To be able to convert music into words, it would be to discover a new language – poetry.

❖

196. Any gossip hides a mysterious evil.

❖

197. To have enough willingness so that you inject life.

198. A balanced man is not between good and bad, lie and truth, justice and injustice. This is called a charlatan, an ingrate, a mentally disordered. A balanced man is who knows what he wants, who knows very well his position, before it appears a situation: either he is good... or he is bad...

❖

199. If life is a gift, happiness is a merit.

❖

200. Little he knows little he does.

❖

201. Sometimes I think that some people exist only to smell bad and to make our life a living hell.

❖

202. We were born so naked that no cloth can hide this little unhappiness.

❖

203. –I am still wondering "what did I do wrong"?! – You are present.

❖

204. Be generous with your things, not the another`s.

❖

205. We cannot become what we want, but only what we are.

❖

206. When we talk about us, we are in an intellectual impasse, because however we put it, we succeed in limiting only to us... becoming involuntarily selfish and defiant.

207. The risk of great ideas is to fall in the hands of little people.

❖

208. Be honest in a quarrel... "do not bring up the past", the great Dalai Lama enlightens us.

❖

209. Tricked by a little hope, I was pierced by life.

❖

210. To feel so lonely that to sleep down, on the rug, in front of your own door.

❖

211. Nothing is even so simple as it seems, but neither as difficult as it is said.

❖

212. The more things you want, the poorer you become.

❖

213. He who sees nothing good is a bad man, and he who see nothing bad is a stupid man.

❖

214. It is impossible not be hated by someone... there are people who cannot do more.

❖

215. We loved each other so much that we could not stand each other... but together.

❖

216. I swear on Adam`s belly... "All my ships have failed"... on a rich island.

217. One of man`s biggest foolishness is certitude.

❖

218. Disappointment is at the basis of everything... that is not made out of love.

❖

219. The courage depends on everything that is done out of fear. Where there is no fear, it is called madness.

❖

220. We all want a better world; only God does not believe it.

❖

221. The dream has become a dream, even for that I do not have time.

❖

222. Suicide is due to a soul attack, after which no one can live anymore.

❖

223. The fact there are people who hate us, is a normal thing. We should make problems when no one loves us anymore.

❖

224. Your smile can become the source of joy of the person besides you, and the joy of the person besides you, can be the source that keeps awake your smile.

❖

225. Do not give choices... you exclude yourself.

❖

226. It seems that, only when I do not have another idea, I create another one.

227. How could we have expressed unhappiness, if we had not known what happiness meant?!

❖

228. For those who lack the sixth sense, nothing comes out good.

❖

229. Like every surgeon I wash my hands before I write something... but especially after.

❖

230. Wanting to end it, I realized I did not have what... but to continue it would be too much.

❖

231. But a death on a run... better on a fight.

❖

232. School is good only for those who study; the others should be taken to a vocational or arts school.

❖

233. We do not get closer or get away from death... it stays permanently by our side.

❖

234. In every good man there is a little wise person.

❖

235. If pharaohs had presumed the way in which they would be shown to the entire world, they would have certainly preferred rather to be immolated.

❖

236. The truth always hides a thing favorable to be revealed.

237. If you do not punish the bad man, he would not hesitate.

❖

238. Honesty honors the man.

❖

239. How easy can a single man destroy an entire country... of idiots?

❖

240. A stupid person is that person who had the bad luck that neither he nor the others realize what is he good at in life.

❖

241. "I will tell people, who you really are"... a simple sentence that everybody fears.

❖

242. The most enemies are the creation of our fake friendships.

❖

243. The bad man usually wins, because he has not had any other occupation.

❖

244. Doubt gives birth to doubt... it does not have place for doubt.

❖

245. As joyful and happy are we when we look at the sun, as joyful and happy will it lighten our way.

❖

246. A first step to wisdom is redemption... through kindness.

247. Looks cannot give you what behavior does not have.

❖

248. "Love is blind" until the first pain, then it becomes immune.

❖

249. If nobody dares to disagree with you, life would not hesitate.

❖

250. On earth there is Heaven and Hell... in the skies there are only clouds and stars.

❖

251. First love is not lived as it is dreamed.

❖

252. –How much it takes you to come to me? – About two hours. – No, no... in money, how much?

❖

253. Today I was surprised that I have not felt until now the joy of the sun or of the spring. It means that until now, it was not the case... I had joys bigger than that.

❖

254. Either you are optimistic or pessimistic; hope is the same for both.

❖

255. Wanting to be an ordinary man, I become nobody.

❖

256. We all search for the good, but we cannot find it all in the same place.

257. We always try to justify our stupidity, but never our intelligence.

❖

258. Man knows many things, but the little he does not know is at the basis of his entire knowledge.

❖

259. God believes in us, as we believe in Him... "in percent".

❖

260. The difference between a smart man and a genius is the fact that one is recognized after tens of years, and the other after a few hundreds.

❖

261. Evil is a degraded good under an embryonic shape, a rock missing conscience.

❖

262. It is normal that somebody thinks what you have said, but it is abnormal that somebody thinks only what you have said.

❖

263. When we talk about us, we prove grandstanding. Even if we complain about our defects, we do not do it freely, but to receive praise for our qualities.

❖

264. Than torturing myself in order to write something stupid on ten pages, I rather torture myself for nothing, and write it on a line or two.

265. Being endowed with so much sensitivity in order to be good.

❖

266. I do not know how others are, for I do know even how I am.

❖

267. Once with the confidence, love begins, too. Once with the love, life will begin, too.

❖

268. Being incredible is a really incredible thing.

❖

269. The person endowed with a little interior richness aspires to a greater exterior richness.

❖

270. "I think a lot" is an impression, which only those who do know what thinking means have.

❖

271. A writer cannot say that "there is no think I have not thought", because the things he will think later will say the opposite.

❖

272. I cannot stop here; there is not my place here.

❖

273. It is said that "hope dies the last" and only after that the real pain follows.

274. The ugly people have always the tendency to render uglier, by all means of crazy things, as brilliant and out of ordinary as possible. If they cannot get the attention the beautiful people receive, they try to shock us by all sorts of bizarre things.

❖

275. When I was little, I used to watch the grown-ups with admiration and respect. Now I am only left with the watching.

❖

276. You shut up or you talk, all for nothing, if you do not think.

❖

277. If we had left on a planet that would have not rotated, after what could we have calculated the hours, the days or the years?!

❖

278. As much as we deserve the good things, we deserve the bad things, too. Otherwise, from where so much power to endure them all?!

❖

279. Seeing the poverty in which some people live, I began to find an explanation for how some other people got so rich.

❖

280. People do not look for happiness, but only for the other people`s envy.

281. The meaning of life is a problem as all the other problems that the man is asking without even having it.

❖

282. I am sorry I do not speak with Evelink, but not as sorry than to ever want this thing.

❖

283. Only by conversation and meditation one can discover its valences, the books can only inhibit with their own.

❖

284. The love in order to succeed in arriving to the heart passes first of all through many organs of the body. For the young people, the path is from bottom to top: heel, sexual organ, stomach, heart... For the older people, from top to bottom: brains, eye, nose, mouth, heart...

❖

285. Where is the tear from the early times, so that I can cry it again, with passion and life, that has so easily melt on my face. Everything I have left is to love, blinded by happiness, I cannot realize very well what or who.

Spiritual Needs

IV

286. It is not easy to be God, and to be surrounded by all the stupid people and caressed by all the crawlers.

❖

287. The silence... when it becomes heavy as lead, not anybody can find its flaw.

❖

288. Even if the man was not bound for ending up somewhere, he was destined to go. And he was so tired of walking, he kept stopping... and there where he rested well, the place he praised.

❖

289. After so many years of searching, I realized I was born at home and no matter how much I would keep searching, I will not find anywhere something more exalting and more beautiful than her.

❖

290. The friend, when you have him, is sweeter than a brother and when you lose him is more bitter than any enemy.

❖

291. Before being afraid, relax, do not get nervous.

292. Rather than a long life on knees, better a short one standing up.

❖

293. They say that "work ennobles you", only that it ruins me.

❖

294. The smile eases your soul.

❖

295. When many people get together against you, you are stronger than them. Everything is not to let them unite to another group, because they will become equal to you.

❖

296. The intelligent man is the one who perceives the things around him in his favor, and the stupid one against him. One is enchanted by the song of a bird, the other is irritated.

❖

297. Even if we do not have what to live for, we always find for what...

❖

298. It is not a big deal to be right, but to make righteousness.

❖

299. When the woman is sad, those who are having fun suddenly become her enemies.

❖

300. Within us there is a point of attraction, for every misfortune.

301. No idea can make us wiser. It only indicates us the point we should reach, the road that totally belongs to us.

❖

302. The fact that we do not have something to live for, keeps us searching it...

❖

303. Subtlety – the refined human's weapon.

❖

304. Be good, but not too good. Be honest, but not too honest.

❖

305. A good punishment repairs, it does not instigate.

❖

306. At the trial, the accused starts a fight, and a few guards intervene, to calm it down. The judge asks again the defendant, but this time very irritated: "Do you admit your guilt?"The defendant roars: "Very well, very well... I admit I am guilty... but who tore my jacket?!"

❖

307. If the orphan until 18 is the person without parents, a orphan from 18 until 36 is the person without friends and from 36 and up is the person without family.

❖

308. When you are good, it hearts the bad man, that you do not resemble him.

❖

309. You search for cheap things, you shall remain cheap. Little you search, little you shall remain.

310. Seeing the donkey that it cannot be a stallion, now it tries to become friend with... himself.

❖

311. We all know what it would mean to have a small or a large piece of happiness, but yet no one knows exactly what happiness means.

❖

312. The peacock is beautiful when it plumps up, and the man when he loves.

❖

313. Do not give everything you can, give only what is good.

❖

314. The weak man stays at someone`s right, and the powerful man stays right.

❖

315. Be patient to your child, otherwise he will not know how to be patient to your senescence.

❖

316. If in the case of the women the prostitution is the oldest profession, in the case of the men is flattery.

❖

317. Gold has value in any form, so is life, too.

❖

318. At genius people even the stupid things they do are remarkable.

319. On earth, no matter how powerful the sun would shine, it could not light it all. When for some people there is light, for others will be dark. God, no matter how good He would be, could never satisfy everybody. When for some is good, for others will be bad.

❖

320. To certain people jealousy can be seen as a sixth sense and to others as a sixth stupidity.

❖

321. We all wait for a day when everything it will be alright. And when that wonderful day will come, we will realize that only one day is not enough.

❖

322. Giving your soul to God, what do you still offer to people?!

❖

323. In chess, as in life, it is enough to make one mistake in order to lose everything.

❖

324. Pride without substance is silly arrogance.

❖

325. –I served half-time in the Army, I am half a man. / - But man, until now you have been a ... woman?!

❖

326. You cannot cultivate what is not native.

❖

327. Stop throwing to me the dead dog, when to you it is all dead.

328. We are all right, but only a few people make it right or take right into account.

❖

329. Being a victim of life, only death can save us.

❖

330. What we do not dream at night, we hope at daylight.

❖

331. Redemption is not a target, but a virtue. Doing good things is something that is right to be done and that is all. When you do a good thing only for a certain reason, it degrades in something harmful for the human soul.

❖

332. Any rule lacking exceptions is a mischief.

❖

333. Exception humanizes the rule.

❖

334. Until now I laughed at people who cried, now is my turn to light at my crying, too.

❖

335. Lacking inspiration, we become the victim of a strong obsession.

❖

336. The infinite attests the existence of a universal freedom, and suicide attests the existence of individual freedom.

337. A deep sigh tries my tear; do I ask too much to love each other as always?! Your sweet kiss is my law and my only master. The cloudy sky with stars, as some slender flashes of joy, directs me to you, the only happiness that flows in my veins.

❖

338. I can enjoy the beauty of any flower during daylight and at a certain time of year, but I can enjoy your beauty anytime.

❖

339. All things have value, only the mind of those who do not see it is lacking value.

❖

340. I have discovered many lies until now, but never the truth.

❖

341. God, wanting to see clearly, how much He has thought good and how much He has thought bad in life, has invented Heaven and Hell. Only that, in the given situation in Heaven will go those for which He has thought badly, and in Hell will go those for which He has thought nothing.

❖

342. Without meanness, you cannot succeed in everything.

❖

343. The capacity of making your folly understood... it can make you a genius.

❖

344. Happiness is strictly about certain interior factors (physical, mental, spiritual) and certain exterior factors

(house, city, state, continent, earth, and universe). When all these are favorable, we lack only one little detail: the wisdom of being happy.

❖

345. Stupid is the one that cannot realize he is...

❖

346. Life is not just as unfair... as man makes it.

❖

347. We all play so well our role in life that one could say it is real.

❖

348. Animals are endangered; soon man will take their place.

❖

349. I do not miss any joy or pain... I pass over all like a bulldozer on fire.

❖

350. Who wakes up too often all mornings, he does not have so much luck in life.

❖

351. There are so many wanting to be a star, forgetting to be humans.

❖

352. You cannot be as intelligent as to have everything, but not as stupid as to have nothing.

❖

353. Without imagination, there would be no creation, without wish there would be no will, without hope there

would be no dream, everything would be embraced in a nightmare.

❖

354. Even when we are unhappy, there is somewhere a happiness that keeps us alive.

❖

355. Everything starts from an idea... and the force you give yourself to it.

❖

356. Living in an illogical truth, our only escape is the logical lie.

❖

357. The man has the capacity to think, defying any universal reality.

❖

358. After I did everything, I only remained the rest.

❖

359. Men live, artists exploit life.

❖

360. Do you know why I am happy? Because I consider myself this way.

❖

361. Business is when both partners leave with a profit, otherwise it is called cheating.

❖

362. As easy as I lost in my life, with all the cards in my hand, as easy I won too, without any card. There is always something more supreme than the rule, and that is providence.

363. From now to then we find anything, think anything, and do anything.

❖

364. People talk about others` stupidities, in order to hide theirs.

❖

365. From time to time, this boring habit of nonsense things will get a final shape at a certain moment, in a miraculous way.

❖

366. By writing I succeeded in destroying the craziness, of every probable thought.

❖

367. Love smartens our instant.

❖

368. In our own agony there is the unique way to know life.

❖

369. God not having knees, does not know the feeling of humility, and the power to correctly judge this life.

❖

370. There is not a big deal to be intelligent, but to be able to create something intelligent.

❖

371. You may think well and end up badly if force is not your advantage.

❖

372. There is a payment of life that has to be given from time to time to the sufferance.

373. At a distance in the inner world of the man, the real love grows, and the false one lowers.

❖

374. I am alive in a delay, when I fill in a complaint, to be me, at that first birth. To Adam, as it is known, I would have only one condition: not to be deprived of childhood. I would not allow this thing to be omitted, because for me, it values more than any paradise.

Terrestrial elevations

V

375. Peace, however unjust it would be, is good (wise) and war, however just it would be, is bad (stupid).

❖

376. The wise man fights with the idea, the stupid man with the gun.

❖

377. Invoking the ancient wisdom, we may see that: blind it is not the one who does not see, but the one who does not think.

❖

378. The voice cannot reach the sky, in return the sufferance cuts its way to the infinite.

❖

379. Unhappy is the one who does not know what he wants from life; the one who knows, follows his purpose... happily.

❖

380. He does not have money to die, not talking about living.

381. When we ignore a stupid person, we commit malice, when we ignore a smart person, we commit defamation, when we ignore a genius, and we commit genocide.

❖

382. The fact that you do not have anything, it should encourage you. Instead of saying: "I have nothing, I am a loser"... it would be more appropriate to say: "I have nothing, I must do something".

❖

383. When the donkey brays, it sings in his personal language the pain of its soul.

❖

384. Once the night comes, everything darkens, even the man`s soul.

❖

385. Happiness cannot get a form but in the past because it is spared by the pain of the present and by its real context. By the passing of time, the memory gives us the satisfaction of a fulfilled life.

❖

386. The pride of dogs is in their tails, and the pride of men, in their stupidity.

❖

387. Master of life, but not of fate, master of thoughts, but not of deeds.

❖

388. Men are not afraid of darkness, as they are afraid of light... that will reveal everything.

389. Do not study to be smart; be smart and learn.

❖

390. The smart and useless man is a thousand times more stupid.

❖

391. In every woman we search the first love... that we did not have even at our first.

❖

392. The pessimist is the person who is 99% right, but valorizes 1% of his life. The optimist is the person who is 1% right, but valorizes 99% of his life.

❖

393. The smart man`s eye speculates (going forward), the stupid man`s eye blocks up in complicated stuffs (staying put).

❖

394. The weak people look for the mistake, the strong people look for the value.

❖

395. A wrong impression on happiness can make us unhappy.

❖

396. It is not so bad to lose, but to give up.

❖

397. The hell is the only place that God created and where He does not exist. These aspects making me understand the fact that I am exactly in Hell.

398. The man does not hide of well, he does not fluff, he does not praise.

❖

399. God, searching for a way to be absolved of evil, created the Devil.

❖

400. Hope is the optimistic rustling of our existential despair.

❖

401. We cannot fight stupidity... we are born with it. We can possibly ignore it or neglect it.

❖

402. Evil is the force of souls so small that we notice their existence only when they do harm.

❖

403. Just as you cannot be everybody`s friend, no matter how good and forgiving you are, so even God cannot be.

❖

404. Do not be sad because you have nothing, have nothing because you are sad.

❖

405. Being against all evil on earth, you cannot become yourself but a Devil.

❖

406. The man was certainly not created to die; otherwise there would be no reason for him to live.

❖

407. I firmly respect the animals` rights. Once, man was an animal, too.

408. When your enemy wants to go, widely open the door for him, do not slam it into his nose.

❖

409. Unjustly harassing our enemy, we will justly lose friends.

❖

410. When you play with fire, you play with luck.

❖

411. The sword avoids the one with a golden mouth.

❖

412. There are so many unhappy and dramatic moments in a man's life, that suicide (by comparison) will appear a simple triviality.

❖

413. The appearance is the one that succeeds in keeping at waterline the fragile reality we live in.

❖

414. Because of man's imperfection the woman appeared, thus creating a total imperfection.

❖

415. Every year, I do not know how it happens; my birthday is always when it should not be. Either I am sick, or I do not have money.

❖

416. From one to ten a number is missing, without which a lot of things will remain wrong calculated.

417. The evil is explosive, and the good is smooth. That is why evil is that fast succession of things that you can hardly enjoy.

❖

418. Without death we would be stone.

❖

419. If we all complained, there it would be no place for everybody.

❖

420. No suicide can protect you from no sufferance... it rather deepens it.

❖

421. Showing the woman you can do too many things in the house, you risk that she does nothing.

❖

422. To the one who has an unfulfilled soul, no place is suited.

❖

423. We keep saying "the woman loves more the money, than the man", and we keep omitting "the man loves the image of the woman more that the woman herself".

❖

424. Once, men idolized the woman so much that they crown her in the kitchen.

❖

425. What is cheap is too expensive for those without money and what is expensive, is too cheap for those with money.

426. That`s it! What can we do?! We simulate the happiness we saw in our parents. Happiness stays in this way a living legend.

❖

427. Man is so awkward in his actions that sometimes I wonder how he still exists. The creator gave the man the misfortune to think much more than his possibilities to know what to do, predestinating him to make mistakes.

❖

428. You cannot do with money what you can do with a good friend.

❖

429. When hope is lost, hate increases.

❖

430. With little one can make a miracle, with more one can make a disaster.

❖

431. If for every one of us life means something... we for life, it does not seem so...

❖

432. Intelligence lacking the notion of good is faked.

❖

433. I cannot be more than a simple search of my being... lost into the moments that come, into the tomorrows.

❖

434. History does not repeat, because we do not know to learn from its mistakes and because people`s vanities have remained the same... petty.

435. Life... as an exercise of good, can become a praise-worthy attempt.

❖

436. Laziness does not chase hunger... but it maintains it.

❖

437. Saying about someone that "he is stupid"... it does not make you smarter.

❖

438. Where the freedom of speech is enclosed, the conscious of man is compromised.

❖

439. Quitting is not a solution... maybe only for losers.

❖

440. Death is the crunch of our life, and then decline follows. But for some people the birth is their unique crunch, and decline is exactly the life they live; they die before they are dead, they live like alive dead people.

❖

441. I was born at 14 years old... when I wrote for the first time. Since then, I continuously live this age.

❖

442. The one without guilt does not smell so right.

❖

443. You have constancy, you have self-assurance.

❖

444. I do not have time to stay, not talking about working.

445. Your faith is unjust when you defend it by meanness.

❖

446. God is equally closed to everybody, but we are not all equally closed to Him.

❖

447. Flowers reveal us how charming we could be, when we will be in love.

❖

448. You cannot search for the originality, because it exists within yourself. You can become original very easily if you become yourself. Every single man has the secret of a unique formula that cannot be neglected.

❖

449. The difference between a writer and a genius?! One resumes what he reads, and the other what he thinks.

❖

450. I am glad that there is still a truth in this world and that is there is none. As long as there will be paradoxes, the truth stays a simple naivety.

❖

451. Into the little trusts great disappointments establish.

❖

452. I have overcome the phase of wisdom a long time ago; now I am at the phase of normality.

❖

453. The shadow is the cross we helplessly drug after us, even a long time after we die.

454. How many times I did not laugh at these jokes. How many times I was not surprised by the beauty of the same sunrise, the same landscape, the same ideas... What can I do?! The time has come for me to start pretending and to live.

❖

455. I am always seized by the absurd. And every time I am helpless in embracing its vastness... then waking myself in my own absurdity.

❖

456. Many people would have loved to be in Adam`s place in order to become the most popular human being by a simple gesture: biting from an apple. Many people would have wanted to be in the shoes of I do not know what great writer or ruler. I would not be happy at all to be in the shoes of any of these people, because they are all decomposed from many years now.

❖

457. Perfection is the thing that consists in the evolution of the same thing, not in its plenitude. A complete thing is no longer perfect because it becomes obsolete... not being able to adapt to the environment caught in a continuous expansion, it will easily degrade and it will disappear.

❖

458. The problem of many people who think is the fact that they are trivialized by their own deeds.

❖

459. Do not hesitate to make decisions despite of all risks because only in this way you will be able to permanently exploit your valences towards a better exercise of

the success. Try to always overpass your condition. You value does not consists in what you are, but in what you could be.

❖

460. The one who does not know to pick up only the pretty side of life deserves to live unhappily.

❖

461. One thing done is good done.

❖

462. What is undone is loosen.

❖

463. Most times, even if we do not have time, we will certainly find enough time to do nothing, and when we have time, we will hardly find enough time to do something.

❖

464. Pain is the reward for our sensibility.

❖

465. Most times we wake from our sleep, but not from our dreams.

❖

466. As long as I could exist... anyone can exist.

❖

467. Sometimcs we live under the sun, and sometimes under the sign of question.

❖

468. Some people can speak to dead people, others not even with the alive people.

469. What you want is hardly heard, hardly found, and hardly forgotten.

❖

470. There are some ideas that deserve, that after them follow hundreds of pages of silence, and others that have to be written one over another, on the same line.

❖

471. In a dream I have read a book that told me the fact that there is nothing meaningless, but only people are mindless.

❖

472. As there is one single day divided between darkness and light, there is also one single present divided between past and future. As there is only one human being divided between life and death, as there is only one dream divided between real and unreal.

❖

473. God is staying and He is thinking even for some thousands of years, before He tells something. There is no wonder that sometimes it happens for Him to say some wise thing.

❖

474. Truth is like a candle lighted in a total darkness, that lightens the things (that you want to see), but which keeps into the darkness the other things (that you do not want to see).

❖

475. Man passes, things remain.

476. "Hope dies the last one"... but it dies.

❖

477. I know too many things to ever pretend I know them all. I know things too well to be able to ever pretend I knew one.

❖

478. It happens sometimes not to be able to do anything else but to hope with all my heart that there is still, from time to time, a God somewhere up there.

❖

479. Time is a big spike where we plant ourselves, one by one, all the disappointments and joys that we have.

❖

480. Behave nicely because is more useful.

❖

481. The one who does not know what to do takes into account the rules, the one who knows what he wants to do takes nothing into account.

❖

482. When the man cannot find his purpose in life, he says life has no meaning; when he will find his purpose, he will say it is not relevant.

❖

483. Happiness is a beautiful fantasy for which it worth living... and we live fully when it happens to feel how beautiful life can be. / Happiness cannot be found as long as you search it only for you. Because happiness cannot be represented by solitude. / Happiness is a form of allergy that we do at certain things and not always at the same.

484. Every time I tried not to betray my feelings, I only succeeded in betraying the reality we are living in.

❖

485. I go rigorously from success to another success since I took failure as an achievement.

❖

486. In every wrinkle is hidden a pain lacking caress.

❖

487. Life is like a white piece of paper given to you and it depends only on you how you will explore it. In this case you must be very smart in order to do something with the paper and stupid enough in order to think that it is also important what you do.

❖

488. If the impossible had existed in this world, many things would not have existed, if any.

❖

489. Everything will exist, no matter what we do or we do not. It depends on us only the proportion of good with which we will succeed in passing over this temporary impasse of life.

❖

490. Reigning on a secondary level, man succeeds in contributing to the development of universal creativity.

❖

491. Life-fired, into an impertinent reality keeping searching for the fantasy of a singular human being.

492. Kindly indebting myself to an uncertain present, this one confesses to me a loyal measure of my existential capacity.

❖

493. We randomly discover a strolling future that robs us by a disrespectful anonymity.

❖

494. The whole world born of a pure exception is still looking to vainly inspire us a hidden rule in the future.

❖

495. Passing over the daily breath, I am waiting, lost in certain beautiful spaces the spiritual reconnaissance.

❖

496. The enthusiasm of a delayed time is draining through our veins, through petrified lightning, a grave rustle sniffs the soul without tears and sweat lacking boundaries...

❖

497. I do not know a soul without a flight not to be froze up by the vibration of a bad thing. It cannot be happiness the one taken out of pain...

❖

498. Walking on the shivers of some complete pains, I give to the sky the appropriate light o save at least my soul.

❖

499. Absolutely supernatural, the word is nothing and still without it even nothing could be... Silence is the calm cruelty of the supreme inutility.

500. Through the field of stars my dreams fly, above the oppressed sky is rising the dwelling of a direct I.

❖

501. Relatively present without fight, even if we do not know what we know, through us life will not miss anything.

❖

502. In the range of inevitable time, a small compromised destiny is crawling. Of the deceit of faint convictions, you are doomed to leave in solitude every day.

❖

503. Free of you I succeeded in discovering the comfortable emotional detachment.

❖

504. Tasting from the vision of some improvised leaks, the expression of the ambitious meat; it needless wants for life happiness without time. The scent of faint dawns wafts me landscapes crucified in a mysterious betrayal. Miming lessons and symbols of gentleness, I pass through terrible doubt: towards what is the passing of world with so many unsuccessful deeds?! As the cunning infiltrations would say, it destroys my bleak view, preventing the mind to ever justify its point.

Still convulsions

VI

505. Everything is expiated on earth, because pains produce the redemption of the sins that belong to us. So, Heaven cannot escape to us; we will actually exceed it.

❖

506. Striking, I am being thrown in the maelstrom of actions without any form of safety, of prevention and I continuously confront with them, not remaining but to stupidly meditate: my own powerlessness. (Anything you would do, the late will become a too late. Regarding his actions, man proving to be a very notorious belated. Even suicide is proved to be overcome by the situation, being a process too retarded to be able to solve anything, once life has already had you and it disposed of you on its will).

❖

507. Intelligence is customized, and stupidity is universalized.

❖

508. A beautiful thought is the dignity of a clean conscience.

❖

509. A nullity cannot think more than itself.

510. I think only a few people would like to praise that they are really people, even if I did not meet one by now. And this because of one single fact: either I do not know yet what a man is or I cannot reconcile with the thought that he could be different?!

❖

511. If God did not exist, in front of whom would we still complain?! In front of the man?! It would be too humiliating for the one doing this. If God did not exist, how could we be able to justify our non-recognition in front of the other people?! It would be too silly not to pretend that here is "God`s hand" or "God`s will". If God did not exist, who would "forgive our mistakes", who would "absolve our sins", how would we have the power, the courage and the nerve to look into the others people`s eyes?!

❖

512. Suicide is the thing that puts in legitimacy the freedom of every man to live or not to live. Thus, life becoming acceptable (permissive) and not categorical (totalitarian). Life is not imposed, but it is shown to us, it is revealed... to everyone`s power and capacity of adapting and comprehension.

❖

513. What would I be more faithful to God, than He is to me?! Why would I have to feel I own Him, more than He owns me?! Does He think that His Heaven can blind the honesty of giving from my soul more than necessary?! I would be so surprised if Heaven was another Paradise, with who knows what other stupid rule.

514. If I were Adam, the first thing I would do in order to be able to live in Heaven as quiet as possible, is that of cutting from its roots the tree from which I would have had to eat, because this thing was not forbidden.

❖

515. I am like most people. I always put bad in front even if it happens after.

❖

516. If God had not told Adam to eat from "that" tree, even if it was banned, certainly that tree would have rotted alone, before Adam could even pass by it. Everything was premeditated. It is as if He would say: "from this tree you will eat... because I forbid you... because I show it to you... because I will light it for you." Anyway, it still is a great mystery how Adam succeeded in doing a bad thing as long as he was not provided with something like this, not knowing "what is bad and what is wrong."

❖

517. Just try to feel things, not to think them, in order to not spoil their native charm with who knows what obscure thought.

❖

518. Without knowing that I am or that I can be, you would have accepted me gradually, feeling you power with your own stubbornness. Without knowing who you are or who you could be, you made me exist to be able to show you my existence.

❖

519. Truth is like a cake... sometimes is good for the stomach, sometimes it is not.

520. Happiness is a beautiful disillusion... and the scent left behind it deserves to be totally enjoyed. Even if we were disappointed ultimately, at least we would remain with the beauty of the ride.

❖

521. I am perfect, in my own way... in my imperfection.

❖

522. If calumny is a crime, than flattery must be punished in the same way as calumny, because it is as defiant and impertinent as the first one.

❖

523. I am permeated by the inutility of anything that I do. And still, I realize I have no choice, I must do something, even if that thing was nothing.

❖

524. Today I wrote nothing. (Honestly writing, I was surprised how easy you can lie.)

❖

525. He died for his life. Poor man... he could not do more.

❖

526. There are things we cannot succeed in doing but once in a lifetime... they are called "success".

❖

527. You cannot conquer love once and for all; it is conquered continuously... day by day, hour by hour, second by second.

❖

528. As wisdom, as double bitterness.

529. What can we do?! We speak... what we cannot overcome.

❖

530. Your happiness cannot be realized but with the help of the others, even if they contribute to your happiness just by the simple fact that they protect this moment of silence.

❖

531. To have is the most important thing. Only doing one thing you can precede the others and that is because this is the normal way of things. Even when you lack any hope, you can be wrong. All the secret of the human genius consists in doing something.

❖

532. Only what you do not know it exists is enough, and nothing else.

❖

533. We see death as something normal and that until it starts being about us.

❖

534. Sometimes I feel as if I were an aborted child, which makes me think that just the abortion is the true birth in this world being abandoned only wicked souls.

❖

535. If the human body had had the possibility to be formed in time, strictly after the way it thinks, we would have lived in a world of monsters.

❖

536. Helplessness is the nature of every finished thing.

537. The one, who lives a whole life and does not succeed to make at least one soul happy, has lived in vain.

❖

538. Vanity is the most supreme thing, even in front of God; otherwise how would we have known that He has created this world?!

❖

539. In the end, if the meaning of life was important, taking into account that nobody has no idea what it is, man would not have had to exist a long time ago.

❖

540. If death had not existed, it is more certain that there would have been people who would have buried themselves alive, desperate to discover something similar to it.

❖

541. Happiness is to aim at something, not having it.

❖

542. How pathetic could it be that everyone could whiten without any sort of merit?

❖

543. There is no manipulation; there is only the caress of vanity. There are no demystifications, but only "re-mystifications"... updated to the times.

❖

544. I would like to condemn the lie, but without it we would become savages.

545. There are two kinds of people: those who have a meaning (to stay) and those who help those people to carry out their purpose (to work).

❖

546. Our life is validated by the single fact that we exist. It does not matter what it is after death: reincarnation, joy, pain or nothing; because life does not depend on what it is after death.

❖

547. Hey, you!!! Reckless war... heroes are only those who live and die in peace.

❖

548. The beauty of childhood grows proportionate with the spiritual degradation of our maturity.

❖

549. Life cannot be considered life from the moment when its first victim has fallen. When the man is born he does not begin to live, but he starts from that moment to die.

❖

550. For the one who will reach to Heaven, I do know how happy this thing it will be for him, when he finds out that the dearest person of his soul is struggling helpless in the torments of Hell.

❖

551. A great eagle whispered to me once: "The purest things are the feelings. Words do nothing but ruin their purity."

552. All the people have the impression they do something and that is because they do not know that nothing has its own form.

❖

553. Where can we live our feelings?! When around us there is terror?! In our heart, under the branches, where there is no time?! ... The world appears in this way... body with opened wounds. The meaning of nature to contrive fulfillments towards the sky rotten by hopes, the earth is giving us the nobles of a bitter light, maintaining the quantity of night with endless breeze sprung in the depths of our loneliness. An ungrateful opposite pours the entire surface of the universe into a mediocre extended moment, and we, as so many hills polluted by the sources of existence, will remain paved in the stark gallop of the air.

Moral rebellion

VII

554. No matter what it would be, there will be never... enough.

Emotional fraud

VIII

555. In everyone there is a little of everyone.

❖

556. From uncertain realities inept illusions are born.

❖

557. The power of the woman resides in the depth of the emotions she manages to exalt in the man`s soul, only by a simple glance.

❖

558. It is no wonder that you are what you are. Life takes into consideration everything you do... it skips nothing.

❖

559. Believing in God in fear is called superstition. Believing in God of love is called faith.

❖

560. I smile and I calm myself down: life is beautiful, everything is to understand it.

❖

561. The smart and unkind is just a stupid person with a university degree.

562. The time will come when what you gave will cherish more than what you earned.

❖

563. Everything that counts in this world would not be possible without a point of strength and spiritual obstinacy.

❖

564. Loving we will discover the merits of the living joy.

❖

565. Disappear, you pain, from my eyes; I am not in the mood for you today.

❖

566. The study without conscience is not possible without the total annihilation of us.

❖

567. You cannot enjoy a normal and quiet life anywhere and with anybody. The places and the people that support your life are fundamental.

❖

568. Hell is not a place where God throws us, but a choice we make ourselves by any fact, thought or desire.

❖

569. Friends come and go, but the real ones stay.

❖

570. Except of being you nothing else worth it.

❖

571. I understand the process of knowledge has a magical charm. Even if in an ironical way it is slightly probable that life may have a logical argument that does not mean it is not worth catching it.

572. If on earth we must expiate our sins, in hell what will we expiate?!

❖

573. Out from dirty thoughts do not come out clean things.

❖

574. Life is useful for useful people.

❖

575. I do not want to believe in God by mistake, but by conviction.

❖

576. Love gives us the joy of living in the vicinity of the most authentic and innocent values of life.

❖

577. There is a lot of truth in a little doubt of opportunity that there will ever be in a great certitude of life.

❖

578. Live the others` tragedies as if they were yours and your achievements as if they were of all.

❖

579. More preoccupied by the life after death that by this one, we will risk losing them both.

❖

580. The importance of life increases or decreases depending on the importance of things you do or do not.

❖

581. The more tragic the pain is, the more authentic.

582. I have not asked God for anything, instead He gave me life. I have claimed nothing from God, instead He wants me to redeem. I just want to be left alone; instead He will send me to hell.

❖

583. You can go anytime you want from a man`s soul, but it is more difficult to return.

❖

584. God has created the man and He made it the master of all things, but not of his own being.

❖

585. All my old sorrows mourn at the gate of my soul, and the newest sit back and laugh at me like stupid sorrows.

❖

586. The problem of democracy is not going from too much freedom, but from too little mind.

❖

587. When I see an interesting thing I need a break... to update and restart myself spiritually.

❖

588. We can capture at any step the wonderful lessons of beauty. But we love more the tragic and the suffocating ones. They represent us better.

❖

589. Every time we think of the opposite of God, we think of the Devil. But God, practically, cannot have His opposite except His own being. God created everything, including the Devil.

590. It cannot be forgiveness without forgiveness, and friendship without friendship.

❖

591. Many people know, a few understand.

❖

592. I am the world and the world is me.

❖

593. Certainly, nothing is certain.

❖

594. Between life and death there is an illusory distinction, like between white and black. Two paradigms of the same world.

❖

595. I feel as if I were not: a temporal and useless infinite.

❖

596. Stumbled on a day, I fall broke at night. I wake up in the morning and I start it over.

❖

597. The real face of a man can be discerned on his friends` face.

❖

598. Life is a cosmic dust, and the man an astral torch.

❖

599. Eager to think, we will face serious despair. We do not have many choices, nor to much to understand.

❖

600. If as individuals we seem different, overall we prove to be identical.

601. I miss myself, the one I am not any longer, the calm days when I could live as I wanted.

❖

602. The entire content of our existential irony corresponds alarmingly painful to a true moral challenge of spiritual self-reflection.

❖

603. I am surely a victim of her charm. The most beautiful memories of my life start with her and finish with me.

❖

604. Beyond the horizon of her eyes it starts my desert.

❖

605. The utility of love is overwhelming. It turns all the useless things of our life... into excuses.

❖

606. As every day passes, our future seems to stay less and untouchable.

❖

607. Time passes and there is nothing you can do; it is more forceful than all.

❖

608. With ambition you do nothing in life. In order to really succeed in something you need a super ambition, a bull ambition.

❖

609. We are what we are. Nobody denies the fact that we could be anything else than we are, but for the moment we are not.

610. Nature teaches us, nature un-teaches us.

❖

611. More moral is more human.

❖

612. The wise men speak, they hear.

❖

613. Love ascends you to heaven. Desiring a reward means falling back on earth.

❖

614. Life does not cease to amaze us. Its toxic nature disclaims any state of physical resistance. Without any hesitation we can conclude many things, but for reasons of safety we do not do it.

❖

615. When we are young we want to change the world, and when we are adults we end up changing ourselves.

❖

616. When I learned everything, I actually understood I knew nothing.

❖

617. How could you believe in a God who has never believed in you?!

❖

618. Life after death is nothing else but the people before you.

❖

619. I will never understand why I am here and not anywhere else or nowhere.

620. I believe in God out of doubt and regret.

❖

621. Sadness attracts attention! Please keep the discretion!

❖

622. Happiness is easy, man is complicated.

❖

623. My thoughts are my arguments and also my only arguments. Even if I cannot accept all the time what I think, I cannot miss the opportunity to know myself and to understand myself better.

❖

624. If we had been Muslims, how sad we would have been because we were not Christians?!

❖

625. Who has courage has an advantage.

❖

626. I am listening Bach. I feel the need of a little intellectual lift before I read Marin Sorescu.

❖

627. A marriage cannot be solid but by a truly excess of spiritual tolerance.

❖

628. Love gives us the possibility to change the wrong impression about life.

❖

629. I try to stay separately of myself, in order to be as close to her.

630. You could rather make an elephant talk than a woman to shut up.

❖

631. Women use to change their look at least twice a year, and men twice a lifetime: when they are blanched and when they become bald.

❖

632. A love that is not publicly assumed, it is not seriously assumed in private either.

❖

633. Between women nothing is lost, everything is gossiped.

❖

634. We are the slaves of our house, car and laptop... We are slaves of everything that we like and we save.

❖

635. Sometimes I think badly, and sometimes I do not think at all.

❖

636. I feel so good that I want to start running.

❖

637. You have not found happiness, yet? Look better in the eyes of the people you love. Their smile is the way.

❖

638. I love you from all the meanders and synergies of my being. Without you I am stunned.

❖

639. Perseverance makes the difference.

640. In order to live in peace, quietly and in a good communion with the world, everything is to except nothing from nobody. Expect at anything, anytime and from anyone.

❖

641. In our house the child is the service meteorologist, when he laughs is a sunny day, when he cries is a bad day.

❖

642. My first book had a brilliant journey. The first month it was in the libraries and the second month, it was in the old bookshops.

Old echoes

IX

643. In the beginning there was darkness; in the end it will still remain.

❖

644. Who has nothing to do and wishes to waste his life in vain, to stay and think about the sense of life, will be completely satisfied. Me, for one, I have reached the conclusion that, the man has not discovered yet the meaning of life for many thousands of years because this thing it is not his problem.

❖

645. If God made the imprudence to be aware of some of the dramas caused by the His wonderful life, would have instantly a heart attack.

❖

646. Apocalypse cannot come because it is already present on earth. It started with the man and it will end with him.

❖

647. Sometimes I stay in order to be able to work, and sometimes I work in order to be able to stay. That is why I

thought that not when you stay you lose your time for nothing, but when you do something for nothing.

❖

648. As a thing would mean nothing, if it lacked all the things that surround it... so is the man.

❖

649. Each one of us, we are happy, more or less, in our own way and this for a very simple and essential fact: because we live. The fact that we do not realize that we are happy it does not mean that we are not. The reality of this fact will not truly be perceived by us until our survival will not be seriously put in danger.

❖

650. I have never been able to mock to somebody else's love and to tell to one girl "I love you" for fear I do not cheat more than I was cheated on.

❖

651. Stay calm! Death is enough for all of us, only the other things are divided.

❖

652. Adam and Eve, the problem of all the troubles. If it had not been for them, it would have certainly been others.

❖

653. Thanks to love, the entire treacherous projection of life will be able to get for us a wonderful meaning.

❖

654. This is what it is. If it could have been different, it would have been, and if it was possible to be different, it will certainly be.

655. For me Heaven and Hell are equivalent to White and Black where I can see nothing Pink.

❖

656. I claim before God to be given to each one of us the right to stay in Paradise.

❖

657. Pascal teaches us that the best bet is to believe in God. But he overlooks the fact that after death, you will probably be greeted by the biggest surprise – that God was wrong. Therefore, in order not to be surprised after death, the best bet is to be good.

❖

658. Many people doubted the existence of Jesus, but no sage man ever doubted His teachings.

❖

659. Beware of him!!! His Bible... it was his heart.

❖

660. Life is perfect, only the approach of life is imperfect.

❖

661. When you think that all things have a limit, an end, you do not care for anything.

❖

662. Life was given to us to be lived and it what it concerns suicide or becoming a monk, we will reach there, too – to run away from life.

❖

663. Under the land of a sleepless night, it is laying a blind pain.

664. The woman is always right... when she is not disagreeing with the man`s will.

❖

665. Friendship is a wonderful investment on long-term, like a stock on an exchange, sometimes it increases, sometimes it decreases. In friendship nothing is guaranteed.

❖

666. I am surprised by the fact how people are bothered and terrified by the thought that it would not be a God. It would have been normal to be bothered and terrified at the thought that it would exist. Let us see them how they could have solved this problem.

❖

667. We are born and we die one by one, so that someone could observe these things... to be no doubt.

❖

668. Animals are the most evolved being on earth... they resigned to the essentiality of this life, that they treat as such, being able to blend in nature, without any stain or reproach.

❖

669. It remains to be appreciated God`s intelligence, but not the wisdom that He inspired to this world.

❖

670. At the dawn of every life it flickers a shadow of happiness crucified in a sweet deception.

671. A rider stops full of sweat near Saint Peter: - Old Man, there is more to Heaven? – No, my boy, there is not more... for the horse.

❖

672. The woman and the man are too different to report their capacities at some common values. A woman loses her femininity if she tries to relate to the abilities of the man. The man also... Between the man and the woman there are no superiorities, but only different ambitions, given by the physical and the spiritual nature they have.

❖

673. Stop looking for happiness. If she must come, she will come alone, as in the case of love. Happiness takes a certain natural state of being, which you cannot induce yourself.

❖

674. When we have nothing to do – we speak, when we have nothing to speak about – we gossip. (We gab).

❖

675. I am not crazy about taking pictures. But, there are moments when I miss the pictures I did not take.

❖

676. At least today is Sunday. This seems to be the best day that happened to me today.

❖

677. "Women grow up much faster than men" from the sexual point of view and, unfortunately, that is just it.

678. A new day, a new trouble. Anything I would be, it seems endangered by nullity.

❖

679. I come down the hill and I go up on the valley. Stranger to all, I am going back the head ahead.

❖

680. The skill of the intelligence consists in always doing other stupid things than those you did before, reducing in this way the stupidity to a simple mistake.

❖

681. God cannot really come to earth, because He is already present here... and that because His structure permits Him to be different than He is – Universal.

❖

682. In the vicinity of every moment of solitude, it appears something necessary... to learn from zero.

❖

683. If you want to "gab" you can talk about life. Anything you would say about it, it is true.

❖

684. Pain misses nothing. It will gain everything.

❖

685. I cannot imagine how some people can believe only in one thing. I believe in everything and it seems not enough for me.

❖

686. Books support all our evolution. Memory cannot be both accurate and comprehensive. The book representing the biggest invention of the man.

687. Mind cannot tolerate pain. Solving any problem will not be able to stop in any way – our inner conflict. The thought of suicide will guide our steps even beyond death.

❖

688. Even if there was nothing in Hell and it would still be awful.

❖

689. Unfortunately, I live. It seems a stupid thing that does not benefit me, but in a impetuous way it obsesses me.

❖

690. The secret of those who become geniuses is that from their childhood inclination towards something, they did not turn it later into a hobby, but into a way of existence, like a daily work.

❖

691. Do not be deceived!!! The lack of vanity hurts more than vanity itself.

❖

692. If nobody has found the meaning of life until now, this does not mean that it does not exist. The perfection of life and everything that surrounds it exceeds the man too much that he cannot realize it.

❖

693. The elixir of eternal life is love. Love never dies.

❖

694. Why did our neighbor die?! – Because he has lived. – I mean it. – Well, I mean it, too.

❖

695. Everything is transient... except for the evil.

696. Men do not cheat, they summarize the market.

❖

697. For irrational reasons, "common sense" depends on no one, which is why many people depend on "their own will"!

❖

698. I am curious to find out. When it will happen to die, how is the thing really: does the death come to get me or the life will leave me?

❖

699. The great misfortune of the man is that he thinks. This advantage he has over the other beings makes him the unhappiest being on this earth. Man developing his talent to deepen his misery even long after it is gone.

❖

700. Desolating comprehensive ... up on the mountains on the coast of thoughts, it startled in me the desperate problem not to be able to come out of life but by death.

❖

701. So where can we get?! I do not know! But ahead of ourselves... certainly not.

❖

702. The reason of a man to live is to die happy. But life is often more lousy than man.

❖

703. As a simple spectator on the scene of my life, I wake up crazy with more things better to forget, than to remember.

704. I am not at all a pessimist, I am a realist. God is not sleeping, He is resting.

❖

705. Madness has remained my only attraction for this life. In the absence of madness everything seems compromised.

❖

706. Born in the presence of long expectations, we will die around the same questions.

❖

707. Life is indeed a disaster. Gradually, it tends to gain ridiculous architecture of the human condition.

❖

708. Sometimes the little wickedness of those around me leaves me cold, and sometimes it terrifies me the serenity with which they succeed in doing them.

❖

709. Do not be worried... more than you already are.

❖

710. With good eyes, good things are seen.

❖

711. Simplicity is a high moral lesson.

❖

712. To my great disappointment, I have not had still the luck to know the failure of any disappointment.

❖

713. Although I feel I will never find out anything, I cannot help but think.

714. When I first found out about the Ten Commandments, I was disappointed. I had already needed the ten repentances.

❖

715. Unable to be quite rich in valuable benefits, we enter the fierce state of religious consolation.

❖

716. There has been a time when I was eager to find my way in life, like all people. But I never succeeded in finding much. Until one day when I realized that it could not be otherwise as long as my way in life is exactly the search.

❖

717. In my soul no whole smile has survived; they have all been infected by a humble pride.

❖

718. A sweet music discovers thousands of hidden tears. Without understanding something, I swallow some tears and I turn westward.

❖

719. All things under the sky are just of reach of heaven and they will stay at its reach.

❖

720. Stupidity is blooming. The rate of growth is directly proportional to the population.

❖

721. Undoubtedly, demagogy is a moral crime. (Demagogy is a crime that should be assigned in "abuse of trust", otherwise it would be only about "abuse of power").

722. In a dark ocean, the prayer becomes light.

❖

723. I stumble on peoples` sad look in the streets. Embarrassed, I look at them like in a mirror.

❖

724. When you will get old, you will stay that way.

❖

725. Silence absorbs everything. We are one and the same, one with the earth.

❖

726. I was born to enjoy a cold shower and a big cup of bitter life.

❖

727. Unhappy with my opinion about God, I do not stop looking for Him.

❖

728. Love is our only wisdom. In its absence, we are invalid, toothless and empty.

Guilty silence

X

729. By every sufferance, man is closer to becoming a miracle, a miracle of existence.

❖

730. If I had been the Creator of this world, every day I would have found something good to change and to correct.

❖

731. Lacking any coherent idea, we endlessly subtilize uncertain depths.

❖

732. One of the thorniest qualms: to fall into the hands of a God lacking remorse.

❖

733. The hypocrisy of life grows from a disappointment to another. The Difficulty of any explanation amazes the breath in huge deficits of the soul. We cannot use honesty too much; the pain would be too big and too unfair in the same time. Either we want it or not, the great battles we will have in the world, will be and will end always with us.

734. I close my eyes to better see the things around me. They are all the same, as if they were not. Everything is unchanged, the things I miss... and that torment me. Close to death everything becomes clear and deep, like a sullen smile.

❖

735. I am used to amaze... by all sort of aberrations; for fear I do not fall into the lust of a bad truth and not to be able to get rid of it very soon. I cannot stand being tied to anything. This thing suffocates me. At least in the spirit to be free, if physically I cannot be.

❖

736. For some people happiness is a stress, for others a complex. For some people, happiness is a form of pride or a show. Happiness is what represents us, the image we want to have in this world, at any price.

❖

737. Without a doubt, my lucky number is zero. It has constantly represented the sum of my actions.

❖

738. ... I will always kiss your cheek, but not your malice.

❖

739. Oh, you coal soul, you burn without a joke. If I were inside you, I would harass you like a dog.

❖

740. To be endowed with so much conscience as to be able to be... at least that part of good that you consider your life is lacking, it would be something exceptional.

❖

741. I do not disagree, I "rethink". I try to evaluate.

742. We laugh with pleasure, when it is not about us.

❖

743. I am disturbed by her charm. The expression of her entire being enlarges the joy space for another hug, which I ardently profit. Like a snake, my entire body became a spiral around it. I devour every millimeter of it, kiss by kiss.

❖

744. Not only when it happened to be scared, where your only moments of danger. Undoubtedly, if you watched in your soul, any smile of yours would die.

❖

745. Being on a small philosophical adventure, I try to restore my way to an acceptable peace of mind. But, with all this, nothing can stand forever. Everything is doomed to failure, including the truth.

❖

746. In vain you are if you do not love.

❖

747. How could I believe in God, when I doubt my own existence?

❖

748. If eight years ago I was a fool in some ways, now I am certainly a fool in other ways, but, as a few years ago, I cannot realize in which ways.

❖

749. Under a shock of anger and rage, I think more than I need. I lost my patience to believe in something. I am immune. I have heard too many words to ever be efficient.

750. Happiness remains a worthy try of spiritual enno-blement.

❖

751. Our friends are the mirror of our soul. Throughout them we admire ourselves and we boast to others.

❖

752. Smiling, she runs her fingers through my hair. With vigor I succeed in staying calm and watch the sky: walking my thoughts to different holy places of her body.

❖

753. Between us everything was by the book. We met poetically, and we broke up mathematically.

❖

754. We are born in order to live... the pathological form of death.

❖

755. Even if we endure with difficulty our sins, we easily make others.

❖

756. Sadness is a satanic state of mental insufficiency.

❖

757. Being at the end of a final decision, beyond indi-vidual provinces drain to cruel stars the abysmal thoughts. Crazy of remorse and despair, the illusion of life will re-main... a sweet consolation and a complete comfort of pain.

❖

758. As an insignificant victim of the sublime perdition, I take refuge into the solitude, far away from any mean reality. The wish to destroy a clear feeling drowns in some

desolate thoughts. Without malice, a vague expression of pride troubles my soul in different degrees of agony. Nothing proves to be nowadays sufficiently sure to our lives. Even love is playing us pathetic pranks, from a disappointment to another, from a person to another.

❖

759. In the depths of my being is draining a whisper crazy from too many cheap days. Without doubt, what happens with me, it happens with other people, too. For this fact, no matter how degraded life would become, its value will never decrease.

❖

760. The future is a dead end of the past.

❖

761. Once I allowed myself to be happy, because I did not understood very well the notion of loser.

❖

762. After he slapped my both cheeks, I had swollen his nose.

❖

763. I cannot stay still. Laziness is too expensive.

❖

764. One of the Ten Commandments of God says it clearly and loudly: "Thou shalt not kill". Unless it is not mentioned in the commandment what exactly you must not kill, it can certainly have a general attribute (do not kill anything) and not a particular one (do not kill people). However, there will be more ... of our wonderful Church scholars who will not dare to admit it. It is natural to be so.

Sausages and stakes are more important in their lives than this aberrant interpretation.

❖

765. Wonder is an incomplete question.

❖

766. The Ten Commandments are just as essential as the seven years from home. No matter if you are a believer or not, without these things you worth nothing. All this keep strictly to a certain disposition of mind and a mental health that no normal person should deprive.

❖

767. Life depends on possibilities... what everyone gets to live.

❖

768. I do not like to neglect myself, but not to bother very much.

❖

769. Thirsty of life, I do not miss any hope; I hunt them all with great prestige.

❖

770. To my great disappointment, given the fact I do not know any way by which I could know how much I really know, I must live on forever... true assumptions.

❖

771. I cannot realize how rational love is. But, I know firsthand that without love the rationality has no meaning.

❖

772. I believe in God, but not blindly.

773. I am not cheap, but only sparing... not only in thought, but only in feelings.

❖

774. Young or old, music helps us all feeling better and... happy.

❖

775. In 99% of cases, the quality of the air is proportionate with the quality of people in that space.

❖

776. During Pythagoras` times the man was the measure of all things, now it is the money.

❖

777. The fact that I understand Universe, led by man, lacking meaning, it does not mean it is lacking value, too.

❖

778. If "love at first sight" could be considered an accident, the romance that will precede it cannot be but a consolation.

❖

779. There is no reason why I should be bothered by the presence of a false friend; with him I can share the joy of false opinions.

❖

780. "What happened to him?!" "He was drunk. He died in his absence."

❖

781. The philosophy represents a gate of access to the real world. That once you entered, you will never get out... mighty head.

782. The waves winnow my memories... chapters of whole novels.

❖

783. Suddenly and wildly, there appear all sorts of things that cannot prove anything. Nothing but time, that has to be very ruthless to fool.

❖

784. I support many, but I swallow little.

❖

785. We do one thing, and another one happens.

❖

786. Frankly speaking, in the cemeteries, the crosses should be replaced by big question marks. Those would be closer to the real meaning of our life.

❖

787. Pain is everywhere. You cannot escape it. We live in its world.

❖

788. In a previous life I was nothing. Now, I have the privilege to be the same.

❖

789. We are not terrified by death, but by its eternity.

❖

790. Lately I am seriously tried by the idea that life is more about organic stimulus than a rational one.

❖

791. The brain is like a muscle, if you do not put it at work, it atrophies.

792. The biggest tragedy of life is to become dependent on human community. Not being able to survive otherwise than at its corrupt and infect breast.

❖

793. I have not a problem with being alone, and sad. I like challenges.

❖

794. I would rather believe in God than in church.

❖

795. I admit... it escapes from the dominant justice of the political game but not from its rudeness.

❖

796. When she does not like to play with me, she plays with my tears.

❖

797. The meaning of life can be anything. That is why, anything can be important.

❖

798. The easiest way to understand a man is to love him.

❖

799. Sadness represents a cerebral syncope that degrades our entire spiritual condition, in an entire process of perversion to a very late humiliation.

❖

800. Every being represents the drama of his dreams (expectations).

❖

801. We have the right o thinking since our birth. The right to speak, we will have to get alone.

802. I prefer to live with my head in the clouds; on earth there is too crowded.

❖

803. Self-reflection distracts my attention: any physical presence keeps alive a mystical sufferance.

❖

804. I respect your opinion, but not your attitude.

❖

805. Without love, life is a nuisance.

❖

806. More or less exotic, I feel alive. In an attack position, I wait a favorable moment to smile.

❖

807. To love is a matter of life and death. The absence of love kills... slowly, everything we have more beautiful in ourselves.

❖

808. Solitude leaves huge gaps in everyone`s life... that will not be filled but by tears and holiness.

❖

809. The philosophy, even if it cannot be everything, has the skill to precede them all.

❖

810. Any simple sound is a call to silence. Any sublime sound is a call to meditation.

❖

811. Suicide is the abstract of some unexpressed feelings or of some feelings impossible to be expressed in another way.

812. In the melancholy of spring, the sky proves to be closer to my soul than the people around me.

❖

813. Music is the only sincere expression of love that can keep in efficient terms the complete authenticity of the soul.

❖

814. From time to time, we will have to turn back to the smile, as to a wonderful spell of the pain within us.

❖

815. We live times when everything is possible, except for the possible.

❖

816. I walk all day, I walk and I walk again: from nowhere to nowhere.

❖

817. By no pain we will not be able to calm down... the loss of the paradise.

❖

818. Happiness is not succeeding in something, but in succeeding in being somebody.

❖

819. Nobody can conceive he could really die. Even the ones that commit suicide hope till their last instant that a miracle will save them.

❖

820. As long as we are tied to everything that happens to us, we are tied to everything that is not happening to us.

821. It is not enough to believe in God. God is not a simple belief, He is a way of life.

❖

822. Success belongs to the audacious people (without too many fears or prejudices).

❖

823. The one who knows not to do the stupid sometimes and the intelligent always has to win.

❖

824. Santa Claus manages to be for the children what Jesus Christ is for the old people.

❖

825. In the power of our spirit stays the resonance of our name.

❖

826. There is only one exception when we can admit that a war would be fair and that is when it is not happening.

❖

827. From my soul, no wound is missing. The loved one took care of it.

❖

828. With patience you starve. Stop just standing there.

❖

829. I am not always me. Filled with exaggerate prejudices, every day I am the victim of my own facts.

❖

830. Nobody will hesitate to help you... to become more stupid.

831. Crawler is the person who never argues and a cad is the one who never approves.

❖

832. More conscious, more present.

❖

833. There is no doubt; malice is a living example of intellectual promiscuity.

❖

834. You cannot take into account something without coming across something else.

❖

835. Mostly, friends come from the good world and go into the enemies' world.

❖

836. The word enlightens the word.

❖

837. Music brings us together and gets us closer.

❖

838. Thoughts come and go, feelings stay.

❖

839. Everybody represents a good opportunity for each of us.

❖

840. Disgust from sunset, endless sadness. Except for the pain, everything is relative.

❖

841. It is all about money. Including the truth is on its side.

842. Do not be worried that I am happy. It is a momentary glitch that will not last long.

❖

843. The wolves howl quietly their pain, without anyone taking them as freaks. People must still evolve.

❖

844. When I am on the verge of not understanding anything, I already feel I understood almost everything.

❖

845. The only religion I believe in and to which I bow with all my being is love.

❖

846. I am not skillful enough to do beautiful things, but I am ambitious enough to stop drinking.

❖

847. I had the fortune to be born... but not for long.

❖

848. The art of speaking: to be able to suggest almost everything, without saying anything.

❖

849. The man has a round head. Thing that cannot stop him to think in corners.

❖

850. No love is similar to another. Each one has something unique, that we remember separately.

❖

851. Before I die I will dig two graves: one for me, and the other for my thoughts.

852. Nothing more abnormal nowadays but to try to prove you are a normal man.

❖

853. I go to sleep hoping that one day I will wake up again a child.

❖

854. There are people pleading for a paradise without snakes or without apple trees. I plead for a paradise without stupid people.

❖

855. Finally from God`s hands have appeared Adam and Eve, and from man`s hands will come out Dust and Powder.

❖

856. Long live the hope! Hope is with us!

❖

857. Indifference never fails. It dries everything around it. Indifference is the most terrible attack at one`s person.

❖

858. I am not convinced that Hell and Heaven really exist, but I am convinced that certain things are absolutely necessary to exist.

❖

859. Nothing is... too difficult for the miracle. Even if in life we will walk on one way, at the Last Judgment, our steps will find themselves on many ways. (imprinted)

❖

860. Help us God, if you can! Are we born in the shadow of Your kindness... or before it?!

861. Being in town, away from any consciousness, I feel the full affront of sadness. I do not even have time to suffer. I complain running.

Mental shipwreck

XI

862. Sadness kidnaps my tranquility. I watch in the past and I do not see anything good in the future.

❖

863. We do not have to worry about our life. This is just a simple problem of time.

❖

864. The truth often comes in our life like a ghost, which scares any exception of ours. For this reason, we love more the truth that concerns the others, than us.

❖

865. We cannot deviate from the absurd. It is a part of our life, by our own very existence.

❖

866. In every man there is a soul that waits to be found, understood and loved.

❖

867. In a serious way we cannot pay attention to any thing, without not being prone to insanity.

868. Even if life were just a dream, it is a dream that exists and that affects us.

❖

869. Every day I do nothing but live a normal fight... against the principles of stress and anxiety.

❖

870. A love once lost will never be fully recovered. It will be like a flower from grandma`s garden, with fresh leaves and sad petals.

❖

871. There are people and people. Every day, some manage to die little by little, and others to rise a little more to life.

❖

872. I cannot be either atheist, not believer, as long as I did not have find God, but I still look for Him.

❖

873. Peace in the world starts with the peace in us.

❖

874. Even if by many ways we can ease our pain... we cannot escape it completely. Pain is a part of us.

❖

875. Nothing is eternal, not even eternity itself.

❖

876. The absurdity of life surpasses any expectation. There are a billion reasons to be good and just as many reasons to be bad. No matter how we dare to be, we will be totally justified. But only that the meaning of man is to be happy, and happiness will never be found in malice.

877. Love has the power to save us from ridiculous... from not leaving in vain and without reason.

❖

878. After four months of siege, I laid down the arms at her legs and I confessed her I loved her.

❖

879. Smile is a form of happiness... like a "hello" or "hi" between two souls.

❖

880. In life nothing is possible without a minimum of effort and pain. And with a little poetical grace, emotional advantages may increase enormously.

❖

881. By the simple fact that we are bad or good, this thing represents nothing but a disturbing form of protest against life... one more disastrous than the other.

❖

882. The usefulness of life beats all our expectations. Until now we took care to kill our time with all sort of stupid things, than from now on, they will take care to kill us.

❖

883. The product of our facts will reach its purpose only by a happy coincidence. The life of any man as much it depends on him, it also depends on the others.

❖

884. The natural size of our soul is in the real size of our facts.

885. The merit of life is that of giving value to the Universe. Lacking life, the whole Universe would stay a simple explosion of stars.

❖

886. It is difficult to always hear crap. The damage may become irreversible.

❖

887. The fear of solitude comes from the fear itself.

❖

888. Those who have good will and pleasure to meet you will do it. Those who do not want it will invoke different reasons.

❖

889. Searching for a pact as reasonable between us and life... sadness seems to be the most plausible.

❖

890. On how zealots some priests are, Thanks God Jesus was a normal human being and He did not have a missing leg (let us say), that otherwise they would have took care we did not have one, too.

❖

891. The entire cyclicality of human evolution is a product exclusively of natural disasters or of human stupidity. More formidable rivals than this one do not exist in the Universe.

❖

892. In order to approach many things, you cannot be but modest in expression. And with thoroughness you can only waste the time that no thing deserves.

893. Every thought represents a force, a multi-cellular centrifugal force.

❖

894. Maybe yes, maybe not. This is the answer of the reality we live in. Without a more comfortable error we cannot affirm anything for sure. As long as we cannot convince ourselves which is the truth, anything is possible and also true.

❖

895. We still have to expect. Humanism is not possible without humans.

❖

896. The feeling of solitude exudes an unfortunate sense of tensed sadness. Almost in despair I try to make a more comfortable distance from my inner agitation. Surely I realize that I really believe in God. I only deny Him from a desire to know Him and to better understand Him.

❖

897. I try to respect people`s sufferance, but not the selfishness of those who cannot enjoy one thing while complaining about another one.

❖

898. The more bent the head is, the easiest to cut.

❖

899. I sprayed in the space, in order to bring myself together and to recompose.

❖

900. Philosophy is accessible to anyone, religion only to the good people.

901. A lot of joys have gathered in my life, that I did not live. They are difficult to conquer. One of them would be the faith in God.

❖

902. Despair is my answer for this life. Any other answer I would try to give, reality contradicts me.

❖

903. It seems difficult to accept that nothing has changed. Practically, those who cried before are crying now, too.

❖

904. When you lose, the disaster would be impossible to stop. Anything you would do, you will not be able to be the same.

❖

905. In this great battle between God and the man, God is not allowed to do anything, man will destroy himself.

❖

906. He asked me:"Why do you live"?! I would rather prefer she hit me, her words fell like two cold drops on my thighs. For a long period of time, I do not want to know anymore.

❖

907. The days of our lives are easily going, like the clouds in the sky: obtuse and confusing.

❖

908. I am tired of doing things for nothing, so I will do the charity.

909. It seems strange I am feeling fine. I have certainly omitted something.

❖

910. The man is not killed by (great) desires... but by (daily) appetites.

❖

911. We can risk our honor to live only on a single purpose: to love. Otherwise we are idiots.

❖

912. Freedom is the joy of any rational animal... to live in peace.

❖

913. I could have been a bad person, but I failed. Those around me proved to be worst than me... they have destroyed me.

❖

914. I do not have to pray, I have the prayer in my bones. Every step is a glorification of God.

❖

915. Nothing can boast a man more beautiful than his own beautiful acts.

❖

916. Water stains only dirty things.

❖

917. After every living model, the waves grow and die under the weight of their welders.

❖

918. The sky?! There is no abyss more steep and deep.

919. I feel empty of any right to believe in God, for which... I believe in silence.

❖

920. The perspectives seem opened to a raid of more painful experiences. It is noteworthy the thankless nature of the human destiny to succeed in changing the world without destroying it.

❖

921. Suffocated by fury, I lost any pleasant source of pride. I am a shadow, the shadow of a lost illusion on earth.

❖

922. Man is doomed to not understand the woman unless he loves her.

❖

923. The man evolution is strange: the things have rather evolved around him, than him in himself.

❖

924. The hostility of life is overwhelming. We cannot remain children forever; we have the obligation to grow up.

❖

925. It sometimes happens to me, too, to wait and think, but many times I think when I am not supposed to and this does not help me at all.

❖

926. Happiness is hidden just on those wonderful places that money cannot ever buy totally, no matter how much it would be: love and friendship..

927. The first steps to wisdom: modesty, moderation and gentleness.

❖

928. Dignity is earned, not begged.

❖

929. It is not a big deal to believe in God, but to prove it.

❖

930. For some people, maturation is a long and slow process, and for other people, it is inexistent.

❖

931. The hunter does not kill only animals, but also the love for life.

❖

932. The purpose of life is life. Everything that sends us away from it, it degrades us.

933. It is not a big deal to write beautifully, but to write correctly. It is not a big deal to think much, but to think fair.

❖

934. In any form we would try to take it, friends prove to be of two kinds: friends and "friends".

❖

935. As long as you dedicate your life to money, it would be dull and sad.

❖

936. Disappointed in life, we deceive ourselves with more vigorous hopes.

937. It hurts me when I cannot give a happy contrast to my thoughts, but it hurts me more when I lie and I try to say something else than what I feel.

❖

938. If you stay hidden, hidden you will remain.

❖

939. We have the freedom to be happy, but not the wisdom to succeed.

❖

940. On holidays we wish everybody "happiness", instead, on our daily life we do not give it to anyone.

❖

941. Malice is a twitch, and sometimes it is silly.

❖

942. It is not big deal to make friends, but to keep them.

❖

943. Love is the most valuable compass of our soul. Without it we would be lost in the wilderness of life.

❖

944. Man cannot be perfect because he is not, but he can become perfectible by kindness.

❖

945. Man`s facts represent a sign of recognition and full identification of his spiritual identity.

❖

946. I smile... and I succeed: pain after pain.

947. I do not know the meaning of man. But man`s purpose is as simple as clear and precise, embedded in the depths of his subconscious: to win at least by the end of his days the pride of his own existence.

❖

948. Being next to the person we love, everything becomes nice and shiny.

❖

949. If all men were like you, it would be Heaven on earth... awakening in the sky the vain of gods that they were not born here, among us.

❖

950. Happiness is everywhere... where love is.

❖

951. The rough fire of sadness squeezes me from the whole light of kindness. Apart from love, I cannot accept anything from anyone.

❖

952. Practically, every time I try to write down my last word, even if in reality I have never succeeded in writing my first one.

❖

953. I hate being right and something bad is happening ... and I`m glad when I am wrong and something good happens.

❖

954. Wandering is good, but not enough: wandering without retrieving worth nothing.

955. Our happiness lies in the hands of those around us, and the happiness of those around us lies in our hands.

❖

956. We must love; otherwise we will not win much from our life.

❖

957. The true love is when it happens to love somebody for no reason.

❖

958. The fact we met by accident did not surprise anyone. The fact that we separated for a really good reason, surprised everyone.

❖

959. "Am I beautiful?" "Sometimes... " "Well, how so?" "Sometimes you are annoying... "

❖

960. Everything a man wants is to have a woman by his side... and if possible, another one every day.

❖

961. Almost everybody complains they do not have money and almost nobody that they do not have a mind.

❖

962. I am the rooster in the house, but she is the mastiff.

❖

963. People do not know to drink. Most often he is confronted with the abuse of alcohol: either he drinks too much, or not at all.

964. Everything is on a crisis. I spend my solitude on T.V. with my grandmother, the pain in clubs with my friends and the joy at memorial services and funerals with my relatives.

❖

965. If I were a stray, I would be a Buddhist, and if I were a breed, I would be a Catholic.

❖

966. I have no illusions. I am a more prosperous man... in ruins and deceptions.

❖

967. Any ardent conviction is an abuse of knowledge.

❖

968. Stupidity seriously harms health.

❖

969. Rather than losing my years "working for nothing", I better win them "doing nothing".

❖

970. You do not know a man?! See who he sits with and you will know who he is.

❖

971. Men have domesticated the animals, and women have domesticated men.

❖

972. The woman has the gift of making the man doing what she wants, immaculating his conviction that those were his wishes.

❖

973. In any obsession there is a deception.

974. In what concerns sufferance, I was wrong. I took it too much into consideration and too little in vain.

❖

975. The difference between your fiancée and any other woman on the streets is the fact that about any other woman on the streets you are certain you know, but about your fiancée you have no certainty.

❖

976. I love you with all my kidneys. For your sake, I will drink in my honor.

❖

977. Guns are harmless, but not the idiots that use them.

❖

978. It happened one night when she threatened me she loved me, and I scared her by asking to marry me.

❖

979. We have a rich country and poor characters.

❖

980. God gives us, and we destroy them.

❖

981. He is smart in his way, but not in mine.

❖

982. I was born in the centre of the Capital city, on the periphery of Europe.

❖

983. I cannot totally believe in God, but only partially: as long as it is good for me.

984. Most often, we only like the truths that allow us to do and to think the same things. Otherwise, we hate and we discredit everything around us.

❖

985. After a year, we accidentally met on the street. We quickly exchanged a glance and two tears. We are both to blame, we are two stupid persons who pretend they do not love each other.

❖

986. I took care to do everything it is important to do in a lifetime. I have not left my old age another task, besides death.

❖

987. Talent is good, but not enough. Professionalism stays an attribute of nuance and detail.

❖

988. Neglecting what you feel, you neglect what you have more precious in you: your soul.

❖

989. I insist on thinking. I comply and live.

❖

990. Love is not misleading, people are.

❖

991. We have equal rights... in life, but not in dignity.

❖

992. Surely a single man finds it difficult to smile. But, if he does not do it, he will risk to remain the same.

993. A vegetable will never be stressed. Stress is the attribute of an active life.

❖

994. With humor, life will easily pass.

❖

995. As the man managed to appear out from nowhere, as well he might disappear.

❖

996. The more you complain the more helpless and defeated you become.

❖

997. You cannot live in a neutral way. By the simple fact that you exist, you are an accomplice to everything.

❖

998. If the universe had had a heart, it would have been the earth.

❖

999. Serve your life carefully and use every moment to learn something beautiful.

❖

1000. Life does not lack anything; it has everything: good-bad; beautiful-ugly. Man having the possibility to find everything he is looking for. You can find miracles if you look for them. You can find disaster if you look for it... beauty, ugly, pleasure, pains. In life you can find anything, but you must want it.

❖

1001. By a careful Cartesian doubt, a lot of new grieves trigger a febrile sentence of solitude.

1002. Shaking me limply in the fierce vicinity of life, I cannot do anything but hope to a very gentle connotation of sadness.

❖

1003. A church is not more sacred than a poplar, a flower or a wisp of glass.

❖

1004. I denounce any victory obtained by bloodshed.

❖

1005. The enemy`s imagination of hurting you has no limits.

❖

1006. A more satisfactory knowledge of the existence triggers a defiant expression of sufferance.

❖

1007. I profit with joy of the opportunity of every free time I have, in order to breathe some life.

❖

1008. I smile and I calm down. From the world full of emptiness, I sometimes succeed n forging some good thoughts.

❖

1009. Life is a true test of temperance, benevolence and resignation.

❖

1010. Using abusively of sad thoughts increases the severity of time.

❖

1011. Sitting down on sand I share with the birds the joy of a common faith: the sky and the sea.

1012. It is important to stay away of the sad waste of time, in order not to confuse with it.

❖

1013. Try to do your best to not leave the good spirit.

❖

1014. The capacity of enjoying life is a spiritual inclination as serious and capital as possible.

❖

1015. For a while I stopped doing mischief to the gods... as long as it is about one who preaches peace and love for people, it represents a god respectable and worthy of consideration.

❖

1016. A man who knows what he wants does not hesitate in doing what he wants. Your life is more than necessary for you to be happy.

❖

1017. In life you actually do not lose anything, unless you give up smiling.

❖

1018. Sometimes I am too weak to avoid sadness. Those who want to always be happy should be proud of it. Joy is a rare quality among people.

❖

1019. The basic ability to survive any being in order to be able to survive is perseverance. Every step in our life corresponds to a desperate need to change and to restart spiritually.

1020. You cannot trust too much in one thing without being wrong and that is because you will lose sight of the rest.

❖

1021. Most often people are not cruel from malice but from the fear of not becoming vulnerable and easily devoured.

Passing vibrations

XII

1022. Sadness to lovers of knowledge, the whole spectrum of understanding easily exceeds the measure of any expression potential. When life ends, the wished-for answers will remain limited ... even beyond life. Fed up with too many evasive goals, we prospect expressive suggestions, in short naïve nostalgias. As we prove to be too poor in spirit to keep the joy alive, each and every one of us expresses the same gloomy fascination for as different as possible types of suffering. Lost on the way to our own happiness, our similar aberrant identity is clear. Having not even the slightest argument for a balance to live, we simply stay and carelessly watch our own decline. The neglect of happiness leads to our terrible identity being customized in a pitiful register.

❖

1023. A more and more difficult relationship of spiritual approach is growing every day. Thousands of thoughts go on and off mysteriously, vainly. In fact, nothing special. Everything seems to revolve dramatically around the same magnificent Universe of "FUCK".

1024. The most interesting part of life is silence, which I greatly enjoy through a long sigh. A wide knowledge of existence exceeds any absurd reality of our mental power. As a triumphant value, the moral rightness has become a general mockery... .In our inefficient life, if we try to pay some of our sins, we'll be turned into stone; the sins will overtake the value of our existence.

❖

1025. Let's admit it! It's understandable for people. But what about animals?! How incredibly important was the rule they disobeyed? Important enough to be sent away from Paradise? There exist so innocent species that you may wonder in horror: why do these beings live this life? How could it have been possible?

❖

1026. With convulsive smiles I realize the noxious essence of some small passive tensions. Huge waves of pains flow towards the sky, projecting in the abstract the magic of some incurable sorrows. In any logical attitude, the sadness appears in so many strange forms in every soul. If life is a bound to the infinity, the pain is the infinity itself. The involuntary disdain provides a familiar landscape to any revolutionary mind, to be able to save his destiny in a defiant as possible legendary echo.

❖

1027. I wandered along an unnatural day and I admire the realistic tendency of the sun to mime a new morning every single day. The past is murmuring an altered joy and it amplifies a specific volume of pure nostalgia. Despite senses, I express an extraordinary passion for new and higher sufferings. A significant measure of rightness distributes high temperatures in the heart, prolonging in the soul a bitter cry of too many lost faith. Nobody has a clue on how incredibly much he loves life before the critical moment of death.

❖

1028. Joyfulness manages to make people better. Only this way, the soul can fire the sweet light of life in our bodies. Have no shame to rejoice, because sadness is a greater shame. I kindly look at the pertness of these lines. How much poetry in such a boring day!

❖

1029. Trying to exceed the ridiculous reality of my difficult spirit, mysterious emotive wings begin to vibrate in a glorious glowing flight. When the emotional intelligence intensifies a variety of specific contexts... .to sadness, high emotions foreshadow in disastrous contrasts. But, for an extremely acceptable recovery of my own spiritual identity, I'm trying to manifest desperate needs of attracting decisive joys only for myself.

❖

1030. Towards the midday ... ... the sun loses some of the morning freshness. Smiles fragmented into space easily capture the overwhelming dimension of the surrounding nature. Every accurate translation of life provides the ridiculous taste of death. In this hysterical atmosphere of uncertainty, the whole logical expression of the human sorrow can be undoubtedly controlled. A serious source of nervous disorders leads to denial of all the honest symptoms that accompany us. Looking for a more accurate expression of the moon, a large sigh of angels will kneel in the depth of our soul. Many people, many aspirations to ... loneliness.

❖

1031. Victory ... is a human paradox. The price is so ridiculous.This can be only a curse or a lyrical expression of our troubled life... The paradox saves life of any purpose or reason to discreetly meditate.

❖

1032. Light is not only what you see and dark is not only how it feels. The decay of happiness in so many selfish sorrows harms the soul with large sufferings.When we are one step closer to divine,it will appear capital ... and need to rediscover how to live.

❖

1033. Bowels of life bustles at the sadness wall with a tiring gentleness. Shaped as an idiot blazon, the ashes of our ruthless hopes lie in various places. Being in a love crisis, we complain bitterly about our vain beliefs. Throughout our whole life we mark the number of tears in values of absolute truth. Damn it! There are nights over which we managed to get through development of high repentance.

❖

1034. We suffer fear and suspicion with a close eye, the explosion of our presence in space. A more rigorous reflection increases the flow of silence in multiple desolate expressions of slander thorny. Ironically we claim a lot without proving almost anything ... nothing gratifying and commendable enough for us or what is around us. (The world we live in has reached a destination outside world ...

Getting to know the human being better; we can easily understand all his existential drama. Nothing is random.)

❖

1035. Amazing universe, more logical, more tragic and absurd as the days go by. It meets everything through exuberant vigor. Lacking any strict location, it allowed itself to get to get stranded in a dark infinity.

❖

1036. Throughout our long history sadness will appear as a great victory. Curiously, we do not treasure life too much, but typically, even if we do not realize it, we offer everything in exchange of being.

❖

1037. The irresistible sadness makes the disdain of loneliness more efficient. As a try- out element, grim bustle emphasizes the blind fear. More carefully, we prospect reasonable ways through which unfortunate injures of the wounded soul could improve isolation.

❖

1038. Through countless gestures, words and deeds, the pain tends to be justified. I feel as if I had already died, that is the reason why death can no longer hide any mysteries from me. Failing to use me death only kills itself.

❖

1039. It is always talked about. Enjoying a glass of ice and a bit of sun, I listen to small glimpses of happiness regretfully. Suave memories cause confusion to my mind and a feeling sweet sleep. The woman's ambiguity, so filled with pleasure and torture, allows its full lecture by a great deal of arrogance ... The smile fits her perfectly. She's born for it.

❖

1040. Do not hesitate to think. Set free the beast within yourself and you shall be free. Freedom is a moral duty of each and single man. Beyond freedom there may be nothing else or at least nothing good.

❖

1041. Meditation offers a unique prestige of free customization of our entire spiritual resort.

❖

1042. I wish I were a grasshopper, a plant or a drop of dew in the middle of a summer morning. There is an indefinable pain which separates me from God, a pain of not of being something other than what He made me, of not being something other than what He wanted.

❖

1043. Sometimes I happen to believe in God because of my good sense to those older than me and smarter. I cannot do anything more. I still do not feel that I am worthy enough for Him. Who knows? Maybe later ... There is still a state of ideological failure between me and God. He seeks unlimited love, I only seek true love.

❖

1044. Our broken heart struggles in tears of ice, not being anything else than a target. Being hit by emptiness with our eyes sharpen by malice, we manage to keep weighing a labile health. And finally, so as not to be totally compromised, we will try to live only with half-closed eyes.

1045. I proclaim myself idiot. I really do not know how much I needed us to know what pain means or what it might use to God to see us in this ungrateful form!

❖

1046. Properly managing the emotional pressure, countless irrational attitudes will be saved. However, because of the lack of clear views, a sad face will remain carved in many of our views.

❖

1047. The human individualism lacks any grounds. As long as man is not alone in this world, it cannot be the only purpose of this world.

❖

1048. The picture of our life is a perfect source of doubt and despair. We have no reasons to doubt. Facing death all our sorrows will gain a shape and a meaning.

❖

1049. Lacking any promising identity, our inner emptiness incites silently multiple rational emotions of full uncertainties.

❖

1050. The irremediable seems to be the definitive answer for much suffering, over which we have no way to go except with the help of some serious after- effects. Comparing the present situation with the one from two thousand years ago all the things around us changed but instead the vanities have remained the same.

❖

1051. Being isolated in the past, I discover in any new beginning, a real bridge to a completely illusory. An extremely unreasonable burden of breaths unbearable which have almost completely broken the balance of light from my bones. Finally, with passion and anger, I will assume my right to life ... lacking any kind of lucidity. Otherwise I do not see anything. Every three seconds I would explode into dozens of desolate expressions.

❖

1052. I've calmed down! In Cişmigiu few snowdrops manage to assure me of the arrival of spring. With eyes full of hope, I think to myself: not even a single thing is too late to start early.

❖

1053. It's getting cold and foggy, but I do not care. Young and full of big goals, I wander by myself between earth and sky, thoughts, dreams and aches. There is not much I can do. Without love, life is a shame.

❖

1054. Felt a lump in the throat which troubles my breathing. Heaven and Hell can only be another way to suffer. Would it have been better if God had created a world in sin and tell man that if he dared not sin and eat from the tree of sin and righteousness would be cast forever in Eden? Wouldn't it have been better if he hadn't created any trees? Wouldn't it have been better if he had been born thousands of years ago and hadn't known anything about this God?

❖

1055. Oceans of humility easily feed the entire indignation of the human existence. The earth torn by the passing of time has supported for thousands of years the same common show, an impartial macabre. No clues about all the things that surround us, our whole spiritual being seems to be insignificant from birth, with an absolute aura for a sadness universal.

❖

1056. Reasons of concern grow inside the illusion of life. The lack of joy we can truly force us... to have irreversible thoughts. On the other hand, depression remains an inadequate response to many of the problems we face. Unfortunately the only logic that we lack in almost everything we do is kindness. Do not tell anyone that is not really what we are feeling, but it cannot always be relevant.

❖

1057. I come to love by accident. Independently and objectively, I take action in full agony. An unlimited weight of joy envelops critical moment in incurable pleasures awakening in me feelings that I have not felt in a long time. I had almost forgotten that I can feel something like this. Happy I confess embarrassed: "Please do not let me be the victim of solitude. I fear myself ... and all the more impossible. "

❖

1058. Horus rose from the dead after three days, and I rose from loneliness after three months. I do not know what it was for Horus but for me it was horrible, almost rotting myself alive.

❖

1059. If we had not lived, we would not have meant anything in this world. But the fact that we live will take a longer period of time to convince ourselves of this.

1060. In the evening, on the deserted streets of the soul, great terrible pains fail to entertain me in some high philosophical nostalgia. Nothing is emptier or meaningless than human wickedness. The whole aspect of the human tragedy itself attracts an overwhelming feeling of guilt. Full of passion, I still deplore the moral weakness of being unable to swear openly out loud, without compromises or idiotic remorse.

❖

1061. Fed up of too many bitter conflicts, each breath seems to become more and more worrisome. Lost in the depths of the soul, like a flower at the edge of the desert, I try to appear confident, devoid of any future, at the criminal calls of the Gods.

❖

1062. Notwithstanding the specific norms of high moral conduct, I wanted to avoid two negative thoughts, but I came across an useless one. So I will quickly take two steps back and I'll start over.

❖

1063. Sometimes I happen to shudder of pain, for more information about the past. But I've calmed down. Somehow or another, I manage to fool myself.

❖

1064. Contempt weakens my mind. Felt throughout the entire physical condition of the soul at a low level. I no longer feel good enough for myself. The reality of this fact embarrasses me .Close to despair, I start to regroup.

1065. Externally, our presence in the world manages to get more and more misshapen tasks. Through a connection to reality, we can develop profound contradictions endlessly. (true)

❖

1066. Floe lead runs through my veins, a feeling of ruthless sensation of fraud and deceit in any illusion there is disillusionment.

❖

1067. The size of each point of view liberates a beautiful challenge in my soul. Do not reject anything, I incorporate everything.

❖

1068. Trying to find a suitable place for myself for some quiet steps. Thoughts discrete joy feed in limited quantities, sensitive roots of generous illusions. Whether we like it or not, so that we are able to understand something from this world, we'll have to go beyond all understanding.

❖

1069. Guerdons of sighs move towards me, smiles full of suspicion. Lacking any landmark, sadness spreads quickly in air. Crushed by too many unnecessary sufferings, I can no longer visualize honesty all my thoughts. But simply as a mediator between life and death, I am haunted by vanity to endure them all. I've got nothing to lose, by the very fact that I was born, I've already lost it all.

Last evasion

XIII

1070. Nostalgia mixes lucidity promiscuous, enveloping the frail soul to a scary vision. Today a good friend is not the one that does something good for us but the one that does not do any harm.

❖

1071. When I approve and believe the figures gives us a scary truth. The disease spreads.

❖

1072. Shaken by too many apologies, glances and disdains I become a victim of disgust. Wickedness shatters human purpose. –Do not believe in it!

❖

1073. Life is an occurrence which tends to the supremacy of a unique happiness ... Life is a quality that vivid cosmic feeling to which every stone longs for.

❖

1074. I do not know how important God would be to you, but I certainly know that the person who you would be in front of Him would be very important. God can be anything and this precisely because He is not anything.

Therefore only a single detail will matter before Him what kind of person you are (good or bad)?! There is no middle way, whoever you are: a non-believer (regardless the doctrine) or a believer (regardless of religion).

❖

1075. Trying to look for a way to rest the end of the universe over love the infinite failed dramatically in the absurd.

❖

1076. The sea frisks over the cliffs. Warm air kneads silently the night. An indistinctive nuisance keeps trying to relax my thoughts dementia. Naked, decomposed and bored, I leak into the rotten sticky light of an early joy. All the stars, one by one, start to sparkle in my eyes. A small joy borrowed from the stars ... which I take with enough idiotic gratitude. As if anything matters in this world.

❖

1077. The denouement of agony blows away entire beauty of the soul. I hate it all ... because of too much love. It often happens that I understand too little mainly because I just thought I understood more.

❖

1078. Inwards an incurable smile stays decomposed. I find in heaven, that solidarity of love that the earth is missing. Yes! Appearance is a sentimental weakness of a distant opinion. Detaching this inner flavor I feel the affront of rightfulness as it reaches its vulgar concept.

❖

1079. Covered in silence, over any kind of pain I start to perceive how far the wickedness of a desire can go.

Frightened by only a few certainties, I gladly take on much more.

❖

1080. Man's path is the gentle stop dedicated to the sky, inspiring to the fickle moment aesthetic instincts.

❖

1081. I carefully live and die every moment. Down because of a moment's madness, I exclaim my liveliness. Judged sometimes as abnormal man seems to be good, too. I lurk politely. Taking the easy life, I dare to hide more answers ... that kept cheating the good parts of the soul. Paying hard the politeness of every joy, the heart splits the moment into two, taking the pain from it. Without any cure, I still love unconditionally the entire world ... the far away world.

❖

1082. In the morning awakenings there is the flesh weakness towards discovering the latest hidden earnings from inside. The misunderstood guilt of living seeks justice through the bowels of small justice, hurting the spirit with empty hopes.

❖

1083. I hide my quiet life fearfully. Sharing someone your view on life will always seem to be the same, triggering the idea of collective punishment. There are several things which we admire contemptuously against the force of good things. Disappointment coldly takes the emptiness refreshing the exhausting light. Gathering too much twitching, struggles and wrongs... you will kill the air smiling. It will be hard to believe that only through this painful suffering of things, we can achieve quality of life. Close to absurd, we will always discover a secret attraction by confronting it.

❖

1084. Still happily I am waiting for the outcome. How important is it to gain a little love?! Carefully I spiritually contribute to the reasoning of my decisions. The sea fixes over the entire surface of the beach a friendly scent. I wake up in love. I feel that my first love was a fake. So I say "this ... this is love at first sight" .

❖

1085. A couple of sighs are willing to measure my loneliness. "I am indifferent. Nothing touches me. "

❖

1086. To me, victories appear to be temporal ...only for the moment. Especially those of despair. Following the own solitude, I begin to discover a embarrassing state of general weakness. My own indolence, degrading offensive frightens me. Bending the ear a damn owl foretells my sorrow. I live too stupidly, too ambitiously, seeking the same things. I hope that the potential of these endless losses will not persist after death. Suffering arouses honor disgust ... and the need keeps the will ... abusing. I start to feel all the pain, crucified by the madness of a moment. The major crimes pass over the sky. Everyone sees them. As if they were some comets laughing at our pitiful appearance. Still trying to reap the fruits of this diffuse crystallized world, we will shamelessly reveal their lack of meaning. What fun and fast to apostrophe the human pain in heaven! Oh! That is the reason why God refuses to show Himself. His smile will betray indolence.

1087. Frightening and overwhelming. When there is fear, I manifest a secret attraction. I admire the way objects fall.

❖

1088. Deeply immersed in the innocence of knowledge, certain temporal acuities capture at a slow pace the passing of life, offering the overwhelming thoughts a favourite annoying voice. The energy of a reasonable time fakes a temporal numbness. Thinking about the past which is exalted by severe contractions, I remain numb because of the eloquent way in which fear can sometimes give off the evidence of being and sometimes the drama.

❖

1089. Endless wounds float directly, maintaining the fresh mark of a hidden prayer. The martyrdom of virtue voids the shattered existence, perfecting the "Inquisitor" guilt, which can allow a divine victory. Dissolving appearances, I admit I am a castaway. In vain, I was far away now. Towards dawn I scream with fear, the reason awakening. The light keeps moving busily in the thicket grieving. The allergy, the fear and the loneliness begin to show themselves in the depths of my soul, an overwhelming meaning: the error of being. In the agony of vast surfaces I see myself completed and also defeated by a petite paradise lost.

❖

1090. Through an involuntarily access through the absolute you can foresee a certain degrading intelligence , highlighting numerous legitimate attitudes ... The never ending surprise, cracks the image of the human condition, accelerating the tragedy.

1091. Complaints stray sniffing the ground in a suicidal thought. The phantom of faith floats randomly skyward as a heartwarming passion of mankind. Formally, I try to maintain the validity of shapes, deepening the drama of a pathetic sigh. It appears that the mystery of survival can successfully sustain the whole ephemeral glow of any soul in flames.

❖

1092. Demeaning our existence by many evils, we live ideally under the terror of a holy empire which also seeks to balance one way or another, the great passions of mankind. Under the cover of dubious reasons, you begin to distinguish the madness of greatness. The secret of inner illusions almost spit in your face the proof of the passing of the time.

❖

1093. A lost hope directs my overwhelming feelings. Without any second thoughts it pushes me towards the middle of the final vision. Full of sad satisfactions the absolute seems to sit in a violent cosmic edifice, irritating the monotonous space with funeral pleasures. The blood languishes some more in the dark passing of time... expressing dramatically the impossibility of fixed fate. Through spirit fever the time slowly goes by indicating the thirst of thoughts in a rhythmic measure of funeral greatness.

❖

1094. Agonizing in too frequent offensive hugs of hope, I am trying to say, to protest and take action. Near, above, living banished away from the green and wilderness. Answers and questions I kept shifting and turning. Applying a wild interest, I create a short drama. Even if the thought cannot always justify its being, the degrading biological life tends to be ennobled by the spirit. Trying to double the final ecstasy, the equivoque, draining by running the picture, the drama will also end.

❖

1095. Hurt by distant transhumance pleasures, I see myself hit by certain pedantic feelings. Living all over gain the pleasant times through so many thousands of struggles painfully created, nothing seems serious. How much indolence: one has to love the good side which opens the eyes. You know, don't you?! By this dark spirit force, I could measure the abundance of absurd formulas. Oh, oh ... Or maybe not. It would be too much. Nobody deserves to die ... more than the one who created it.

❖

1096. I cannot disagree with the guilt of a single absence. Not even his. Contradiction shatters the neutral regime of any being, by doing the makeup of a hostile imperialism to each and everyone. In an altered form, a smart enough belief so as to reduce the man to silence.

❖

1097. As a poor man I love secretly. My eyes are pierced by the edge of a retreated sea withheld from his warm steps... sizzling love and awkwardness. Dashing in the anxiety of these female shades I feverishly revise the rythmicity of some lost caresses. Its absence can stun the world ... to frenzy. I still carry with me the last minute of a too late a smile that could have brought us together.

1098. The desirable use of a forced faith can produce bitter spiritual conversions. In the depth of human innocence, the persons who commit suicide may seem amateurs. As an irreversible product of nature, inside of which there is the divine desert.

❖

1099. The pathological form of knowledge can awaken science of the last sacrament. Resisting evil you will resemble it.

❖

1100. Starting the romance you will complete the tragedy. In agreement with an improvised walk love still dwells on her lips. I become a flame, a stray embers ... kept alive by love and spasms.

❖

1101. Over the decades, huge conspiracy will precede the mystery which keeps covering the bleak reality. Suffering serves to fulfill the necessary amount to any being to be able to achieve "appreciation". Indignation still deeply exists creating an abyss in every killed smile. "The truth exists" as unacceptable and unjustified as ever. Carefully I refuse salvation. No one else can deliver justice to another through somebody else's justice. The will tends to keep awake the consciousness, providing discipline to some appreciable disdains.

❖

1102. Rejecting the stiff terms of the world, I am trying to leave as much free space as possible in the universe. I admire how stubborn animals cross all the earth, only through a mere cry. They do not stumble in words, full themselves, they do hurry in this life.

❖

1103. Tearing up the tears from the pride of doubtful passions one may distinguish the legacy of our only greatness: happiness. The process of responsibility of an obvious reasoning illustrates "stunned" the convenience of every mistake. Everywhere the sky keeps trying to take over the discordance of exalted hatred on earth, by inducing a feeling of a cursed process of honor. The reality's problem seems to be played in the same supporting roles. Continuous positive claims of the spirit, illustrates the rigor of a moral injunction: contempt cannot maintain than self denial. That's indeed a disappointment.

❖

1104. It is fine when others bear the burden of life. The degrading punishment of life produces terrible riots to every soul. Longing for freedom the man came out of the cave. Disappointed by too much freedom, they will go back.

❖

1105. As an unconscious expressed in pavement of night, I breathe artificially calming intensities. Temptations and lost hopes in space, protect and crown the mind ... inciting spiritual independence to a deadly organic jump. The reasons of love taken admirably support those voluptuous which may create sparkling forms even to the most draconian darkness.

❖

1106. Admitting hierarchical concessions I returned troubled to a sigh moment. From the bottom you can notice the mountain and from the top the emptiness. Contrary to appearances, nothing is what it seems, but surprisingly, they really are.

❖

1107. Great joy, great misfortune. Felt disproportionately love maintains profitable ridiculous inclinations from somebody's behalf. Often the only friend who can fight alongside you, better ... against you.

❖

1108. The legitimacy of hatred seems assured when we discern life. With so many unfulfilled riots, earth is still troubling, perpetuating severe contradictions. We do not give up! With such commendable cynicism we accept the injustices of survival inspiring the soul tragic reflection of cowardice and dishonor. Only through the desirable destruction, freely consented, we carefully maintain a natural born faith to obtain the divine mercy, even a minimal gesture.

❖

1109. A syndrome of proof, the truth transforms hope in such a way so that it can enable the entire moment dedicated to the mortals. The violently created suffering transforms rigorously the desolate darkness towards the same dead point. Due to unfortunate representation of life, I continuously discover my limits. Among so many hidden reasons, a sick demonic thirst keeps trying to save my soul, conceiving frequent happy concessions. Surprised, I find the whole human favor, being worn every now and then by honest smile. Okay, okay but in vain. Just out on the street, I perceive freedom as a bigger cage.

1110. Organizing discussions with different realities, discussions selectively oriented carefully developed can closely monitor their own residues. In the depth used of any used purpose there is some selfishness: mediocre and dull. I wander randomly the horizon of sadness, prevailing the vanities of the last forceful purposes. I refuse the discipline of great triumphs, of the human "wickedness", reclaiming the quality, not the existence.

❖

1111. I 'm sad when I notice so many outstanding trifles. Being unable to explain the potential of a rational ending, the spiritual climate keeps trying to project benefits included in fierce cadence of destiny. Finally stopping, a cold rain of thoughts, I find most virtuous the light of joy than then light of Gods. Unable to justify its purpose clearly, life can be felt with each approach a constant sense of bitter legitimacy. Only by respecting life, you get uniformity in the horizon of understanding the things. So forget it ...

❖

1112. The sun comes out at dawn below the senile sea level. Above the beach there is a dripping noise of sad noise waves. Seagulls regularly betray an incurable grace managing to look good in any season. The basic flexion of used thoughts often tends to provide important components for understanding other types of awareness than rational. Doomed to death by the most basic suffering, movement manages to maintain the eternal destiny of the world.

1113. Covered in an irrational anger, my body still shelters perdition. However, it would be impossible for me to ever leave the tear of these places.

❖

1114. Excited by the general expression of protest, a lot of time left in evaporation stresses my emotional struggle towards a bloody melodrama deeply generous to capture in a way or another the lost time. A strange mixture of love a shows the basic features of any logical obstacle, prevailing a clumsy significant pressure: life is nothing to understand but just to live.

❖

1115. Addressing the declaration of a supreme statement I still seem to be afraid of that temporal stopping of will which could endanger the personal responsibility towards everything that is around me.

❖

1116. The birdsong successfully cools the air, providing the first effective option to a small hope of slow calculus. Being in the mood for a pleasant transfer time pleasing I seize the prospected abuses in the past, discouraging any anger result. Carefully managing kindness, we could "perform "life at a high level. That's it! Fallen into this poetic project, the metaphysical report lists the moments of sheer excitement, suspended in short gloomy depths: the nature admiration confers prestige to the sublime sadness, proving an inherent bodily detachment.

❖

1117. It is too easy to decline the simple reputation of being. It is unfortunate that in the face of a basic abstract sense to honor his religion, man tries to get corridors just in heaven, and Divinity manages to pull out a winning hand from any wicked war.

❖

1118. Nothing to forget is not forgotten. Lost in my own life, I often meet a fresh pain tide. There is nothing I can do. With age, my pain tolerance decreases. Maintaining the existence of some strange sadness I continue to develop vain sensitivities. On the orbit of self suffering, the threat of a drunken smile appears because of too many formal pleasures. Humiliated by so many abstract features I live now and then, when I have time ... a sinister freedom divided into multiple slaveries.

❖

1119. Bored, I admit my disappointment more and more often: the benefit of life, based on the prejudice seems unfair . There are situations in which interest runs inhuman, in the name of every idiotic goal. A sufficient number of dedicated individuals aspire more and more often to only one desire ... to be fulfilled all the time, continuously. By our nature of losing everything, the difficulty appears to extract the hidden life light from each and every one of us. Remarkably, we can get over everything ... with or without a cause. Thus, certain adorations start to give way to filtrates: I refuse to have the right to die taken away and be replaced with who knows what obscure heaven or hell. Being robbed by the flow of past hidden sorrows, whatever I do, life will remain the prison of the open doors.

❖

1120. The wild irony maintains a miserable joy. Tired of wandering so much life has moved on too much ... so I have it from the distance. Even if the day goes by, I find myself less and less; the sun manages to amplify the simple joy of living.

❖

1121. Dragged by so many high expectations, I still struggle to understand what I have never understood: Why do we live? To move from here to there, a while and then die? What is the logic in all this?! Anyway, you need to have an enormous indifference to accept such a thing and no kind of logic.

❖

1122. Under direct effect of a bleak analysis, the eyes seem to penetrate the spirit of raw reflections. We live for the fame, for sex, for money, for anything but what we really should – to love.

Self Publishing România este o platformă online dedicată
publicării, tipăririi, promovării şi distribuţiei naţionale
şi internaţionale a cărţilor autorilor români.
Orice autor care publică la *Self Publishing*
îşi poate vedea cartea în librării în 30 de zile şi mai puţin.

Intră pe site şi publică-ţi cartea sau scrie-ne pe adresa
suport@self-publishing.ro

Comenzi pentru cititori, librării,
biblioteci, depozite de carte:
distributie@self-publishing.ro
tel. 0740.531.108, 0740.531.284
www. self-publishing.ro